Considering Horsemanship

A Book of Ideas Inspired by Two Decades of
Harry Whitney Horsemanship Clinic Journals

Tom Moates

Other Books by Tom Moates:

Discovering Natural Horsemanship
Round-Up: A Gathering of Equine Writings
Six Colts, Two Weeks, Volume I
Six Colts, Two Weeks, Volume II
Six Colts, Two Weeks, Volume III
The Christian Horseman's Companion
Mane Thoughts
The Old Sleeper, A Spy Novel

The Honest Horsemanship Series:
A Horse's Thought
Between the Reins
Further Along the Trail
Going Somewhere
Passing It On

Considering Horsemanship

A Book of Ideas Inspired by Two Decades of
Harry Whitney Horsemanship Clinic Journals

Tom Moates

ISBN 978-0-9992465-8-0
Cover photo by Carole Hess
Cover design by Tom Moates

Backpage photo: A horse named Sunny and Tom riding against the sunset.... Photo by Jaime McArdle

Contents

ACKNOWLEDGEMENTS

Many thanks to Harry Whitney for spending the bulk of his life working to teach others what he has discovered to be true about getting better with horses. Thanks to him for trying to answer so many of my questions, for his patience with my inquisitive nature, and for reading through the drafts of these chapters and providing feedback as this book took shape.

A huge thanks goes out to my horsemanship lesson clients and clinic attendees. Many chapters in this book provide a glimpse into how much my own experience with horses has been broadened by working on horse challenges together with you folks and your horses.

The photos in this book were taken by me except where otherwise noted. Thanks to those whose pictures I am delighted to include to accompany these chapters.

Thanks to Emily Kitching over at *Eclectic Horseman* for giving me some wonderful pointers and much appreciated help as I worked through the cover and book layout for this print edition.

And finally, my wholehearted gratitude goes out to you readers who make the writing rewarding by being an audience, and being an audience because, like me, you're thinking about how to build the best possible relationship with your horses. Thank you for supporting my independent press. I sure wouldn't go far without you!

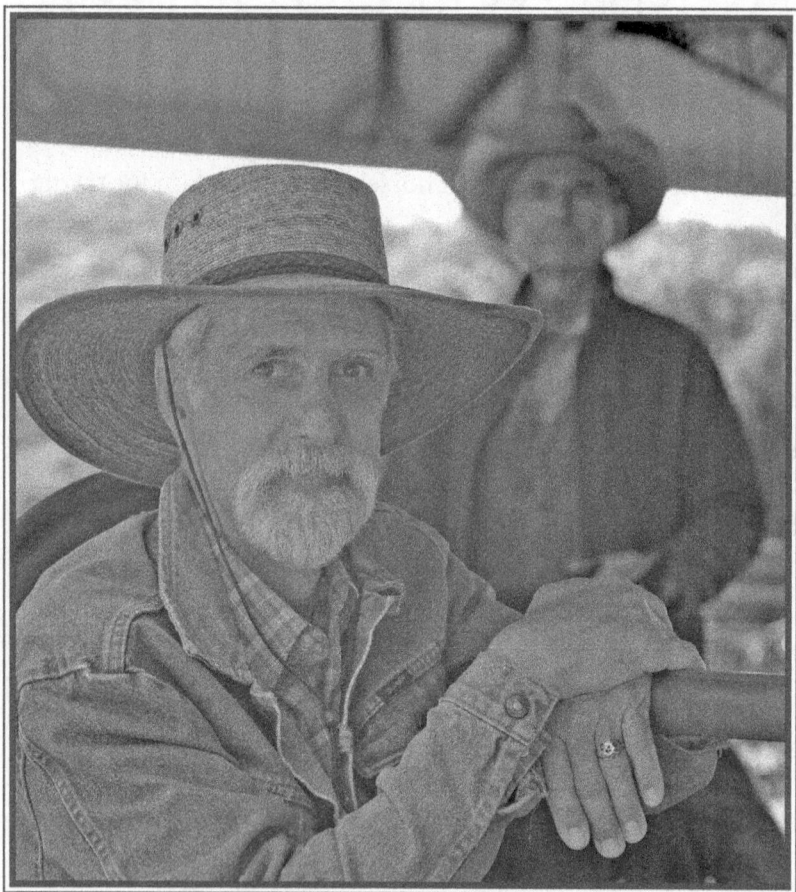

I take lots of photos at clinics, but I rarely get pictures of myself at clinics—so many thanks to my good friend and saddlemaker Jamey Wilcox for snapping this photo of me at Mendin' Fences Farm during Harry Whitney's intensive format clinic in early May 2022. You ever get that feeling there's somebody sneaking up behind you...(on a horse)?

INTRODUCTION

Nearly two decades ago I threw caution to the wind and splurged for a plane ticket; I took horsemanship clinician Harry Whitney up on his offer to visit him at his new place in Salome, Arizona, for two weeks of clinics. Our phone conversations to that point about horsemanship had been fruitful for me, but as Harry said, "It's hard enough to discuss some of these things when we have a horse right in front of us to help us see what we're talking about...."

The journey to get there from my home in the Appalachian Mountains of Virginia proved to be horrendous—missed flights, overnight delays, frayed nerves, extra expenses. I nearly said heck with it and went back home. But I stuck it out, drawn forward by some curious desire to learn from this man with whom I only had spoken on the phone.

As an equestrian journalist, I'd interviewed plenty of celebrated clinicians and horse folks who all had their particular ways of addressing horsemanship. There was, however, something very different and special about Harry's way—a thoughtfulness, a quietness, a humor, a genuine interest in finding just the right words that might help me to understand what he was saying—that spurred me on to meet him and see for myself what the things we had discussed looked like with real horses.

That trip radically altered the trajectory of my life in many positive ways, more than I can ever recount on the page. It was the threshold into a whole new world that has since opened up for me. Now, I can't imagine a life without the friendships, knowledge, and even a livelihood that followed as a direct result of that first encounter. The horsemanship aspect of that experience was summed-up in the beginning of the first book I completed after that trip:

"Hanging between two reins is a thought," I heard Harry Whitney say.

The statement proved profound for me. Profound in its truth and simplicity. It pretty much wrecked everything I'd been working on for a couple of years with horses.

That book, *A Horse's Thought*, has reached a large audience over the years. I'm very grateful it has been read by countless horsepeople who, like me, are doing their best to get things going better with their horses. And that book was just the beginning. Four subsequent titles in that series flowed from me as time went on (*Between the Reins*, *Further Along the Trail*, *Going Somewhere*, and *Passing It On*) that continued to chronicle my obsession to get better with horses under Harry's patient guidance. Then there came, the hefty *Six Colts, Two Weeks* trilogy, that took eight years for me to complete and walks the reader through the one and only colt starting clinic Harry has ever done or expects to do. Most recently an anthology of my equine essays, *Mane Thoughts*, was released, some of which had been previously published in horse magazines.

It has been an incredible ride since that first meeting with Harry, and through all of it from the very first day I arrived in Arizona in 2006, I have kept extensive notes in clinic journals about what I have seen, heard, and experienced. Going to Harry's clinics has been a winding horsemanship trail that has led me all around America numerous times. The journey has allowed me the opportunity to meet all kinds of people who are, like me, obsessed with getting the ultimate foundation in their relationships with equines.

The clinic journals have proven to be very helpful in providing me accurate information from the clinics I have attended while I have worked on the books. And I continue to fill new notebook pages with wisdom and scribbles as I go to each new clinic.

Some years back, I began to crack open these time capsules of great horsemanship for reflection and insight. What I discovered was that many pages are filled with quotes from Harry along with my impressions of what unfolded at various clinics that still grab my attention. But rather than just causing me to reflect back to those times to reminisce as I expected, these notes often caused me to think more about what I'm experiencing right now, today.

Each note documenting what happened at those clinics in the past seems to have a strong, more recent counterpart—a thought that relates to my own horse work and the lessons and clinics I'm teaching today. This realization provided the idea for this book. Each chapter begins with a Harry Whitney quote taken from my collection of clinic notebooks. These horsemanship nuggets get me thinking, thus prompting the chapters, each one being an essay on some aspect of horsemanship as I've learned it from Harry and my own experiences with horses.

I sincerely hope that you will find in reading these pages, as I have in writing them, some answers and thought-provoking questions to consider. The horsemanship journey continues as far and as deep as we choose to pursue it, with horses possessing seemingly unfathomable depths of potential. The better we get, there they are, those equines meeting us at that point and simultaneously challenging us with the next opportunity to improve with them. It's a heck of a ride!

Tom Moates
January 2024

CHAPTER ONE
Locating the Horse's Mind

Thursday, May 26, 2011—Mendin' Fences Farm,
Rogersville, TN.

*"When their minds are somewhere else and their feet are
captured here, things get busy," Harry Whitney said.*

This quote from Harry, like most short quotes from him in
my clinic notebooks, was jotted down in haste and relates to
what was going on with a horse in the moment. It also captures
an important essence of horsemanship as Harry teaches it.

For the most part, the notable Harry quotes I have collected
could be left alone to do their work on the equestrian's
consciousness without any embellishment from me. Nowadays,
however, these nuggets from the notebook often get me
thinking about how Harry's teaching has been applied to my
own learning experiences and to situations in the horsemanship
lessons and clinics that I teach. This one is no exception.

Seeing a jittery horse jigging underneath a rider is quite
common in the horse world. It is uncanny, however, how still a
horse can become when her mind gets right with her body. The
change from a busy piaffe to a calm stance can be instantaneous
(even if only for a few moments) if we get big enough in some
way to break the spell a horse is under which separates her mind

from her body.

The idea of a horse's mind leaving her body being the root of many horse/human issues is unique to Harry as far as I can tell. It is a strange concept for sure to someone uninitiated with how Harry talks about horsemanship, and how, when working with horses, he pays careful attention to where a horse's thoughts are at any given moment. But it makes perfect sense when you begin to think about what he means and when you observe horses interacting with humans.

Just visualize a horse who has trouble being removed from his buddies and placed some distance away from them in a round pen. That horse may run around, call out to the others, push his chest against the panels on the edge of the pen facing the others, and so forth. To Harry's way of thinking, that horse's mind has left his body and is outside of the pen over with his friends. Thus our clinic quote:

"When their minds are somewhere else and their feet are captured here, things get busy."

The horse's "feet" (and the rest of her body) are captured in the round pen, yet her mind is over there with her herd. The result is one bothered horse who shows it by being "busy."

This concept is essential to understanding why a horse acts as she does and is central to understanding the reason why horses get tense and experience anxiety. Tension and anxiety are reasons horses are unable to go along happily with what we humans ask.

This makes me think about the myriad gizmos for sale that are designed to mechanically hold a horse in place per our wishes. Trying to make a horse obedient through the use of devices that inflict some form of pain or pressure to put a stronger stranglehold on the poor creature do absolutely zero towards reuniting her brain with her body. They only create a more intense desire in the horse to separate from such confines however possible—and often the only available option is to go away mentally (much like me when I was in school, but that's a whole other matter...).

Harry's above quote is very revealing and helps me to think about what is really going on with a troubled horse. But it is the opposite of what Harry said here that points us in the direction of fixing this situation—that is, helping a horse to truly feel better inside and to relax and be okay with us humans. The other side of this thought might be stated:

"When her mind is with her body, she is calm."

The question then becomes, so how do we help a horse reunite her mind with her body when she is "getting busy," or, how do we help prevent such a separation in the first place?

Not long ago I came up with a good way to help a client of mine understand and feel how getting a horse's mind back into her body brings about a positive change. The horse was a young gaited mare with an extraordinary ability to have about eighty thoughts per second. Her owner had stepped up to the challenge of getting this horse mentally with her. She had made very good strides towards getting big enough to break the mare's mind loose from other things in the environment during groundwork some of the time, but it was a huge challenge to hold that attention for any length of time if the mare was the least bit tense.

The owner was working on riding the mare during a lesson and the horse was really struggling to get with the program. The mare turned her head and her eyes looked over in the distance, she stepped, then she looked over there, then peered down the hill, then stepped, then glanced over at the neighbor's, then she wrung her head, then sniffed the ground...it was non-stop! I encouraged the rider to try a few things: get more of a forward thought in her to offer the horse, think about a kind of urgency as to where she wanted to go to see if the horse would pick up on that and take an interest, and I even had her slap her leg while in the saddle to work on getting the mare to let go of those distracted thoughts and be mentally there with the rider.

The leg slapping had an effect that I think showed clearly what Harry was talking about in the above quote. When the rider slapped her own thigh, the smack caused that little mare to stop all her busy behavior, direct her ears and attention on the rider, and be mentally present *in her body* for a few seconds before going back to doodling around. In that nano-moment, a quietness came in her.

When she let go of the thoughts of being everywhere else and checked in to see what that big slap in her immediate environment was about, she quieted. It was so momentary that I wracked my brain for a way to help the owner better break her horse's mind loose from being elsewhere and bring it home to her body for a more extensive time so she could have the chance to feel what needed to take place—that she could ride the mare when the horse's mind was in her body and she was lined out going somewhere with an interest.

As we continued to work in the yard, the mare kept jigging and doodling about something fierce. I got an idea and went over and picked up a flag and shook it slightly. The horse was familiar with the flag from many previous groundwork sessions, so I wasn't worried about her spooking. When I shook the flag the horse instantly quit all the "acting up" and focused on the flag. It took very little effort. Next, I brought the flag up close but out in front of the horse's nose, not allowing her to touch it. Her curiosity sucked to it like a magnet to metal, and she drew towards it with a strong longing to feel it with her nose.

I began moving the flag out in front of her, and just like

magic everywhere I led with that flag the mare went with an amazing captivation. In a perfectly calm but intensely interested way, I drew the horse with me anywhere I wanted to lead her around the yard with the flag.

The mare's mind had returned to her body—or at least as close as the flag, which was pretty close. It was right there with her and thus with me, and there was no worry or busy-ness in her body to see while we played around there.

"Do you feel that?" I asked the rider.

"Yes!" she replied.

"That's what we're looking for," I explained, "to see if we can get her mind and body reunited and with you in the riding. We want you to be able to direct her thoughts this willingly from the saddle."

This carrot-on-a-stick demonstration with a rider just occurred to me in the moment that day and wasn't something I'd seen done before. It is a good example, however, of how I have taken important ideas from Harry's teaching and applied them to different situations. By thinking about how to get the mare's thoughts in her body and yet go along with the rider, I improvised and had great results with that little demonstration.

Of course, this situation hardly solved the problem for the owner. It merely provided an example that she could feel of what was possible with her horse. It proved that the little mare could center her brain in her body and go along a line in a relaxed and enthusiastic way with a rider on her back. But what about directing this kind of change in the horse from the saddle? That was what we needed here.

The key to her success would have to be getting the horse's thought back with her body from the saddle—like with the leg slapping—and then be completely committed to staying big enough and consistent enough to let that become the norm rather than the exception. It sounds like a simple concept, but with a quick, busy-minded horse, it's a real job. To start towards that, I decided to try something else that popped to mind. I had the owner stop her horse in a corner of the yard. I went off some distance and placed the flag on a deck by the house. The streamers were hanging off the edge of the deck enticingly, flowing in the slight breeze.

"Now see if you can ride her straight to the flag," I suggested.

Off they went and the mare made a beeline all the way across the yard for the flag, never wavering in her mental desire to go to it and investigate. That was more along the lines of what we needed—having the rider instigate the going and the where to go, and the horse going along with her. We talked about the possibility of having several points of interest around the place to which she could ride the horse. The hope was that she could have her horse's mind present and be able to direct it to here or there or there and use the mare's natural curiosity and interest to have her line out and go in a relaxed and straight way to many different places orchestrated by the rider.

Our time was up for that day. It was easy to visualize the difference between mind-there and mind-gone with this horse. More importantly, the rider had been able to experience the focused calmness of mind-there with her horse from the saddle. Feeling that horse line out between the reins and be straight through her body while being ridden to a point of focus across the yard without crookedness and drama was its own lesson.

This makes me think of times where Harry rides a horse in a clinic, gets some nice changes, and then the owner gets on for a ride afterwards. It is an education all its own to feel how things can be with your own horse just-post-Harry. Such examples help people get a sense of what they need to be shooting for.

CHAPTER TWO
Auto Pilot

Wednesday, October 30, 2013—Harry's Place, Salome, Arizona.

"She'll move her feet to accommodate this but not move her mind," Harry remarked from the round pen.

This quote perfectly depicts that Harry's approach to horsemanship hinges on horses' thoughts—that his awareness of the presence of a horse's mind (or lack thereof) is central to his work with horses. It spotlights the understanding that a horse can interact with humans while *not* being truly mentally engaged with us—and it points us in the direction of asking what problems this kind of mental not-there-ness can cause.

The "this" Harry referred to when he spoke the above words was a feel he presented on the lead rope for the mare in front of him to look off to her right. The horse quickly stepped her front end in that direction with a kind of reflex reaction to the feel presented on the halter rope, but the mare did not look in the direction that she was stepping in.

The previous chapter discussed a horse who was so bothered and busy that she couldn't stand still. That horse's thought had jumped outside of her body and had left the scene to be elsewhere while her feet (along with the rest of her body) remained trapped in another place. This new quote of Harry's speaks to a different kind of mental disassociation where the horse's thoughts in this instance were going deeper within her mind rather than staying present and being focused on the person.

This mental situation produced a different kind of foot moving business, too. Rather than a prancy piaffe as in the last chapter, the mare in this case gave Harry precisely the movement he was asking for. Harry asked for a step to the mare's right and that's what he got. For so many horse folks that would be the end of the matter. As when driving a car, they steer with the wheel (rein) to go right, and the car (horse) goes to the right. End of exchange. Horse's body manipulated. Happy person.

But in this case—as in every case with Harry—he does not ask for movement without looking for the horse's mind to be engaged too, and indeed have her mind thoughtfully leading the way for her body. Sure, in the above example at this clinic he got the step to the right as he asked, but he did not really get what he asked in that he asked the whole horse, mind and body, to step to the right. What the mare did was make her move with what I have come to call "auto pilot."

Auto pilot is when a horse throws some movement out there when a person begins to make a request. To placate the human she doesn't have to pay attention to what is really going on or deal with what is being asked. Sometimes, as in this case, the movement can be exactly what the person is asking for. At times when this happens, it can be tricky to discern whether the horse truly thought about the movement before or not—and one can train oneself to better understand, feel, and observe the difference between mind-there and mind-not-there. In other cases of auto pilot, a horse just throws some total nonsense out there that has no resemblance of what was being asked.

A very good example of auto pilot happened to me with a horse recently that had me about half giddy when it was done because it was a real kick in the pants! A horsemanship client of mine has a herd of ranch horses from out west. When I began working with them, one of the things I played with was riding a couple of them in the round pen, asking them to go forward and take me somewhere, but not directing them with the reins in any way. It is a fun thing to do to see how they will search for answers because so many horses I work with never have been allowed to have any real input into where they go when a rider is aboard.

This particular horse was an amazing, athletic little cutting horse type of fellow. He was super easy to ride anywhere and I'd even call him the dead-brokest horse of the whole bunch. But he clearly had never been asked to go forward and take a rider somewhere without being micro-managed by being directed with the reins. At first when I asked him to walk on forward with the reins down and disengaged, he seemed just plain lost. I had to urge him onward to prove that I meant for him to go even though I wasn't providing any contact on the reins.

Well, he just kind of made a circle right back to the gate, which is pretty typical of what most horses do when I start this kind of thing—they go to where their strongest thought is: the barn, the pasture, away from us...whatever they desire that is through that gate. So I had to urge him again to go on and take us somewhere and certainly not get stuck at the gate. The next thing that happened is what had me laughing so hard....

This horse went into the most amazing reining spin you've ever seen! I nearly was swept out of the saddle sideways in the tsunami of centrifugal force, so unexpected was the maneuver.

But I hung on, quickly made sense of what was happening, and finally had to use the reins to block his thought of spinning so that we could try something else before I passed out and fell off anyway. Every time I'd ask him to go forward without directing with the reins, whizbangweee!, we'd instantly go again into a most amazing and dizzying spin.

That is an example of auto pilot. Granted, the example isn't a perfect match because this little gelding was searching for an answer to the dilemma I had put him in, namely that he go take us somewhere that *he chose* in the round pen without parental guidance, while the mare Harry was working with in this example was not searching at all. Rather she was avoiding any mental interaction with the person. But, the little cutting horse provided a good example of auto pilot because it shows how when he got confused or worried he just threw out the best thing that he knew to do per his experience. That, unusual though it was, just happened to be to spin around his hind end for all he was worth—when in doubt, spin like crazy! People must have proven to him that it was always a praiseworthy maneuver, and he must have figured it was his best bet to stay out of trouble when he wasn't quite sure what to do.

So back to the mare at the clinic. In a sense, what she was doing was the same thing that we discussed in the previous chapter—the horse had her mind elsewhere rather than being attentive to what was taking place with the human in the vicinity of where she was. The difference in this new case, however, was that the "elsewhere" was to withdraw mentally inside herself rather than think "out there" somewhere.

I've learned from Harry's clinics over the years how to see both of these situations. The horses' eyes can tell a person much in this realm. Horses don't usually separate the main thought they are thinking from where they are looking, so if the horse

*Harry interrupts a horse's auto pilot circling of him by walking toward
the horse with the coiled up end of the lead rope in his left hand
during a clinic at Mendin' Fences Farm in Rogersville, Tennessee on
June 11, 2013. (Photo: Olivia Wilkes)*

is thinking some distance away you can bet that is where her
gaze will be focused. Interrupting that can be something akin to
stepping in between a child and the television during a favorite
show.

A horse who is mentally withdrawn can get a glazed over
look in her eyes. That may or may not be something easily
noticed at first. But a clear indicator of this situation is that
the horse will not look in the direction you ask her to take an
interest in—as with Harry's example here, when he asked the
mare to step to the right, she did not look that way. In the
pasture, the wild, or wherever they may be under their own
freedom, horses typically look in the direction they are traveling

unless there is another strong thought elsewhere that grabs their attention that becomes a primary interest or concern while they are moving. But, it seems that during horses' interactions with humans this phenomenon of not looking where they are going comes into play a lot. We humans can be a major stressor for horses that causes them to feel the need to go elsewhere mentally rather than deal with what we present.

It is easier to see where a horse's mind is, or isn't, from the ground because we can see their eyes easily. From the saddle we must depend more on feel to know when a horse is not present mentally. I have heard Harry refer to mental withdrawness in a horse as "going to la-la-land." The horse is thinking of knee deep grass in a pasture full of her best buddies, he'll say, rather than thinking about what is happening with the human in the moment.

One of the things I find so interesting about Harry's approach to horsemanship as it relates to horses' thoughts is that once we recognize and address this issue—that is, get big enough to get them mentally back to the present with us—the horses feel so much better. It doesn't feel good to them to experience the need to disassociate from their immediate environment.

And so, the way Harry handled the mare in this situation was to slap his chap with the end of the halter rope. It sounds simple, and it was. That was all it took to break the spell. She came-to and focused right on him. When he asked again for her to look to the right and he saw she was headed for la-la-land, he repeated the slap. Harry simply did not allow the mare to go to that withdrawn place in her head.

She increasingly relaxed, and in the short time of that session she began to give a nice strong look in a direction Harry indicated and then step there in a thoughtful way. She let down the tension she was packing before by several degrees, too. The positive results Harry achieved by consistently working with the mare in this way let me see how a person could help support a horse to make this thoughtful kind of interaction much more of a habit and a way of life—that it could be carried into other areas of what we might ask a horse to do with us.

I find Harry's approach to talking about where a horse's mind is or isn't focused to be quite amusing. The idea of a horse's brain not being in the moment when activity is going on (can you just see a whole arena full of horses and riders suffering from this dilemma?)...well, it is easy to imagine that things might look pretty sad if horses' minds are not around when we go to do things with them. Well, precisely! When stated this way it seems like a no-brainer that people should begin by considering where the horse's mind is before taking on a task, doesn't it?

Yet it happens the other way around all the time, and most of the struggles people experience with their horses boil down to this simple truth. Why our natural tendency is to try to mechanically force a horse into obedience rather than address where their minds are focused is a real curiosity to me, and I am sure I'd still be woefully ignorant of where my horses' thoughts were if it wasn't for the clinics I've been to over the years where these notebooks were filled. (Thanks again Harry!)

Here's a bunk house meal time discussion at Harry's place in Salome, Arizona on February 26, 2013, a familiar scene where I filled a great many clinic journal pages over the years.

CHAPTER THREE

Fleeing Forward or Thinking Forward?

Monday, September 26, 2011—Bible/Horsemanship Clinic, Floyd, Virginia.

"A race is, 'Who flees the fastest,'" Harry said.

This little quote that I jotted down during a clinic years ago may not seem to say much at first glance. However, I recorded it because it struck me as being plenty profound. In so few words, Harry summed up how a great many of the equestrian population think horses should operate, and at the same time he is hinting at how this notion is misguided.

When Harry said this, he was making the point that many people drive horses' bodies around. This idea ran counter to what he was demonstrating and explaining to us—that horses can be mentally present and follow a feel offered by a human, that they can *think* about going forward (as opposed to panicking and running forward, even if we want to ask for quickness), and that equines can move themselves forward physically and mentally with us in a relaxed and willing way without being forced and/or worried into it.

For instance, it is common to see people put pressure on horses towards their rear ends to get them to move forward, especially when asking for speed—essentially bringing out their flight response. An extreme case of this is a horse race. Whichever horse is driven to flee the fastest wins, as Harry points out. But, this is true in part because the entire field of them are being driven forward.

Which brings me to another quote I've heard Harry say often—"If a horse isn't feeling his best, he's not performing his best." Thinking about this, then I wonder, what if there was a calm, relaxed horse in the lineup of a race? One who was willingly with the rider, thinking forward (rather than fleeing forward), and able to truly collect himself and feel in top shape about running? How much better might he perform than the others?

I certainly think about the likelihood of a horse who is handled Harry's way—mind with the person, relaxed, willing—living a more happy, productive, and healthy life. The mental and physical effects of being forced to bring up that adrenaline along with the poor posture of going with an alarm all the time will break a horse down prematurely. It is well known and no surprise that these kinds of stresses can cause a range of health problems and injuries.

Ultimately what we have in this simple quote is Harry shedding light on another instance of how people cause, allow, and even encourage horses to separate their thoughts from their bodies. It is pretty easy to see that a horse that is fleeing is thinking far away from where his body is (like the "busy" horse in Chapter One) and is racing to get the body to where the mind is thinking. Until the two are reunited, turmoil reigns in the horse's body and mind.

Reflecting on Harry's quote brought back a vivid picture in

my mind of an experience I had some years back—the first and only horse pull I ever attended.

Two things really stood out about the horse-pulling event for me. The first was the magnitude and beauty of the amazing behemoth draft horses. I had never been around horses of such gigantic proportions before.

In particular, the teams of Clydesdales impressed. The shear gravity created by their massiveness when they got close to me emptied the breath from my lungs, and their dinner-plate-sized feet connecting with the ground caused an earthquake as they walked by. The effect on me was much like when I saw the Grand Canyon for the first time. Sure, I had heard my whole life about how huge it is, I had seen pictures and videos of it, and I had been expecting to go see this massive hole in cut into the earth. But in spite of all that, I was not prepared in the least for experiencing the magnitude and the pure WOW! of that great wonder when I walked up to the edged of the precipice for a look... getting up close to a team of harnessed Clydesdales was like that.

The other thing that stood out at the horse pull was how these draft horses were handled. It proved to be one of the saddest examples of horsemanship I'd ever witnessed that the drafthorsemen displayed for the public that day.

I'm guessing from what I observed in team after team at that event that such handling is the norm and not the exception for horses in these pulling competitions. A high level of anxiety already existed in them as they entered the arena, no doubt a result of past experiences and "training." No attempt was made to help the horses find any relaxation or okay-ness in this situation. As they were driven out onto the track to be attached to the sled for pulling, the high heads, bit biting, prancing, and such increased all the more. It was all several men could do working together to position the teams on the straight dirt track and then back them up to the sled.

The moment the pin was dropped into the tongue connecting the team's harnesses to the sled, they tore ahead in an anxious, sweaty, wall-eyed run for their lives. I watched the crews of people working with each team to instigate a frenzied panic in these wonderful creatures as they sought to pull their loads. It was a chaotic scene, and such was the fervor of reckless anticipation in the horses of hearing the pin drop at the moments of hitching, that some teams bolted before they could be connected to their loads. They charged nearly the length of the run before they could be stopped. Backing them up again to the sled became a doubly difficult chore at that point.

I left that place with a strange haze in my head, somewhere between amazement that such incredible creatures as these still existed in our internal combustion world that day and disgust at how they were handled.

I remember saying to my wife Carol as we drove back up the mountain towards home, shaking my head, "If I was the king of the horse pulling world, I'd make some new rules, and I'd begin with: every team must calmly approach the track and back up to the sled to be hitched, and then stand there quietly for at least 30 seconds before being asked to pull or they are disqualified!"

I've told this story a few times over the years and in reply I've heard rumors from a handful of folks about this horseman or that one who has a team that is perfectly calm and that they out perform all the others at such events. I'm not eager to go to another horse pull to find out if it is true, but I hope it is. And if it is true and the others are losing to these fabled, careful, thoughtful handlers of horses, then the mainstream (from what I could see anyway) sure does not seem to be working on enlisting any of their secrets.

I think we can broaden the idea of "race" from Harry's quote to include horse pulls easily enough, but we also should understand that the "race" part of the discussion is not the real point of it. Harry was not worried about racing per se, rather he is addressing how people so often bring up the flee in a horse to achieve forward movement (or any movement), and that is the lesson here.

If we do something as simple as chase a horse out into a circle around us to make it longe, that is the same thing as a jockey whacking his race horse with a crop in the butt. It is extremely common to see people swing the tail end of a lead rope at a horse to get him to step out and go circle around them, for instance. This rope-swinging move is a mainstay of natural horsemanship videos and clinics, to be perfectly honest. And yet, folks simply could offer a feel on that lead rope for the horses to go with to see about getting them to step off and begin to walk around them.

Perhaps people don't believe a horse can accomplish that task without the encouragement of something to get away from. But, we do the horses a disservice by not presenting the chance for them to hear a soft request to go with—to give them that chance, persist with it, and let them search and find that interactions can be smooth, relaxed, soft, and sweet between us.

Harry has helped me to see with absolute clarity that we do not want to offer our horses reasons to get away from us, even little reasons. As creatures with a strong hardwired ability to flee, horses are all too easy to encourage to flee from us.

The quickness with which people can get horses to go forward by driving them into it is most likely why this practice has become the standard of horsemanship. In natural horsemanship circles, this is often referred to as the "pressure" part of "pressure and release." And while a mechanical application of pressure and release which engages the horses' flight response gets quick results, we should consider how a horse feels about that versus providing them a feel from us to go along with.

I agree that it typically takes more time to set things up initially to get a feel working between a person and a horse than it does to chase them into some movement, but once established, what a difference there is to see between a relaxed and willing horse—a reality that then can last a lifetime—as opposed to how a horse feels and postures himself every single time he goes to get away from the person, day after day, year after year.

CHAPTER FOUR
Preserving the Search

Saturday, May 14, 2016—Intensive Horsemanship Clinic, Mendin' Fences Farm in Rogersville, Tennessee.

"Horses are born searching," Harry said. "We take the search out of them."

The prospect of working with a foal or colt (or any horse inexperienced with humans) is both exciting and worrisome to me. On the one hand, I love working with them because there is a purity and an innocence that they possess. They are horses uncluttered by the debris of past exchanges between human and horse.

In this virtuous condition there exists the horses' natural tendency to search that Harry refers to. They take in everything about our first encounters and process it all, cataloging their initial interactions with us humans for future reference for the long haul of life. Most often, a horse unfamiliar with people desires to check us out with a curiosity and openness, and they can intuit and grab ahold of things so quickly it is amazing.

But on the other hand...they can intuit and grab ahold of things so quickly it is amazing! You know, the other kind of things that we do not want to put into a horse—the ones that got in there accidentally because we did not realize we were setting them up.

We sometimes miss or otherwise neglect to acknowledge those first moments when a horse reaches out to us and wants to say hello and see what we are about. Pretty quickly, they can see that their open greeting was not recognized or did not work out. Once that moment is missed, they may not offer it again, or at least not to the same extent that they did initially. I put a heavy weight on the responsibility of making the best use of those first chances with a horse when I am working with one. And, one thing I hope to do is keep that natural tendency to search alive.

Of course, some horses come into the world with a larger dose of natural inquisitiveness than others. But a horse who hasn't been introduced to people presents us with a once in a lifetime opportunity to make a good first impression and carry that forward. As Harry is fond of saying, "So they're started, so they go," and our introduction is the start of the start.

Setting up a search in a horse is one of the most basic elements of Harry's horsemanship. It is not only a good place to start working with them, it is the place to begin. This holds true whether or not the horse is unfamiliar with humans or knows about them all too well.

Often, humans get so busy working on getting something they want from a horse (obedience of some kind like forcing the halter on and starting them to lead by dragging them around) rather than seeing where horses' minds are. Let alone do we spend the time to establish introductions in such a way that a horse can begin to search out what we are asking for, follow a feel we present, and take comfort in our relationship in tiny ways that then can grow into bigger opportunities.

Most horses who have had experience with people are more difficult to work with than those who have had no experience with people. This runs counter to the common view held by many who assume that a "wild"/untamed horse must be the most difficult of all equines to deal with. For example, the country seems to be enamored with mustang starting clinics these days. Part of the appeal is that the word "mustang" conjures up a horse with a maximum level of difficulty to work with—they are wild after all. What Harry says here, and my experience with less-handled horses, points to the very opposite as being true.

The reason behind this truth is simple. As stated above, a horse who is unfamiliar with people is curious to learn about us and has no track record to cloud the relationship. But a horse who has had people experience has absolute convictions about what people are like that cannot be un-experienced.

These convictions often are the very hurdles we face when trying to forge a better relationship with our horses. I am not saying they cannot be overcome and that things cannot work out great—they often do. Indeed, much of my horsemanship work with the public is proof of that. What I am saying is that if we set things up right with a horse from the very first experiences he or she has with people then we can avoid putting people problems into them in the first place.

I've heard Harry tell a story about being interviewed by a journalist years ago. In their initial conversation the interviewer asked Harry a question about abused horses. Harry stopped her and asked what exactly she meant by "abuse?"

She replied, "You know, abused horses."

Harry followed up by saying that actually he wasn't sure what she meant so he didn't feel like he could answer her questions if he wasn't sure exactly what they were addressing. The interview ground to a halt.

The next day the journalist called back and asked Harry, "So then, how do you define abuse?"

Harry answered, "When you leave a horse mentally confused, he feels abused."

That story has stuck with me and I reflect on it often. Humans do a great injustice to horses (unintentionally, but real nonetheless) by being inconsistent. Inconsistency creates confusion and is a major player in horse problems.

And here's the rub—the most important thing to be consistent with is asking that horses be attentive when you present something to them, allowing them to search for what it is you are asking, and then presenting a "thank you" (release, sweet spot, whatever you want to call it) when they hit the mark.

Without the horse's mind being present in the moment, the horse isn't really there. If the horse is focused mentally on you, then you have a chance at getting some real with-you-ness established. If the horse's natural curiosity is taken into consideration as well and nurtured, then we have both their primary thought and their personal drive to investigate working with us.

Once the horse's mind is on track, we should allow them to search. This means we should not put a strangle hold on their choices but let them explore their options. If we are asking for something from the horse, there is an "imbalance" as I like to call it between the person and the horse—a "feel," a "pressure," an "ask." That imbalance is felt by the horse and she or he begins to work to rectify that situation and find balance again.

When they are getting "warmer" in the search or find what we are trying to get them to do, then we present the release/"thank you."

If we do not present a request the same way each time, if we do not release for what we are looking for from the horse each time, and/or if we are sloppy or have no idea ourselves what we are asking the horse to do, then that can be the source of tremendous tension in them. That is the basis for Harry's definition of abuse.

Mirage, my mare, has been a huge challenge for me (as discussed in some detail at the beginning of my book, Six Colts, Two Weeks). She is very strong minded. I discovered that when I would ask her to come along with my idea and it wasn't her idea that she could get as big about pushing her thought over top of mine as any horse I have ever seen. Rearing, striking, threatening to bite, penning those ears—she kept all of her options on the table.

It is interesting, however, that she never gave me the impression of being a horse that was hard to get along with. I never saw this behavior as I worked with her from a foal until she was two or three, and I began working more extensively with her and began starting her under saddle. But the thing is, I had never really asked very much of her before then. It was only when we began to try and do more serious things together in her training that we hit The Spot. The Spot is the point where push comes to shove and she either needs to yield her idea and go along with mine, or I need to yield mine to her.

In retrospect, the reason for this situation was two fold. She was born with the tendency to be strong minded, so this potential came into the world with her. More importantly, I allowed the seed of this behavior to germinate and take root. In small, seemingly insignificant ways that I had not even noticed, she learned she could talk overtop of me in our conversations. Then when it became very important for her to let her thoughts go and search out mine, rather than hearing me and going along with the feel and idea I was presenting, she just shouted louder for me to listen to her. It was a huge and pretty dangerous mess at that point.

At a clinic a years ago now, Harry had to begin to break through this problem by getting bigger than her to get a change in this pattern. After some memorable round pen sessions that involved intensive flagging and watching her walk around on two legs, Harry coached me on how to stay ahead of this trouble with her. That lesson included convincing her to let go of the slightest thought that pushed back against me before any escalation could take place.

The experience taught me many very valuable lessons, including that it is essential to get horses in the habit of letting go of their thoughts in all instances and settings so that they are available to find and go along with what we present, and this needs to become a way of life—one that can build great confidence in them about us and alleviate their anxieties.

Most recently what has happened with Mirage is what really related to Harry's above quote. All during Mirage's starting under saddle, I had her pastured with a few of our other horses—Stoney, Jubal, and Festus (three of the usual suspects from many of my other books)—in a sizable pasture at a farm that had no round pen or other small fenced in space. All of our work had to be done out in the open. It all went pretty well. Then early last spring I decided to bring her back home to the house where we have a round pen and I could easily work with her on a regular basis.

I discovered that I had a huge problem with Mirage. When I asked her to go forward in the round pen during groundwork I was met with reluctance—ear penning, refusing to move into the trot or lope, and then returning to the dreaded Spot mentioned above. The lack of forward in her was palpable when I rode her in the round pen as well.

At times I seemed to make progress with this dilemma, but things really were not clearing up so I decided to try a different approach. I began saddling Mirage and riding her around the yard outside of the round pen here at home. She is a curious mare and I thought about using that to my advantage with our current problems.

One thing that was going pretty well in our relationship was the establishment of meaning in the reins. I had been very consistent getting her thought to come through to whichever direction I indicated with a rein, thus that was one area where she did let go of her thought to go along with what I was asking. Out in the yard, I picked things in various directions that interested her (which wasn't difficult), directed her thought to them with a rein, and then released to let her go there.

It worked a trick! And the beauty was that there were 360 degrees of interesting things to captivate her around here. Not only were there seven farm roads and tractor paths leading into the woods from our yard in all directions, there was a paddock with Niji in it, a grape arbor, a fenced garden, the house, a barn cat, a birdfeeder, a shed, a dog kennel, a tractor, round bales, and on-and-on. Anytime I chose to pick up a rein and ask her to leave the thought of where she was headed, there were plenty of new ones to choose from to enthrall her interest and send us on a new line of inquiry.

In no time at all she was drawing so well to all points on the compass that she simply offered to pick up a trot to some favorites. I just went with that at first. I'd check in and change direction at the trot sometimes to see that she was still with me and she always responded willingly to the rein like she had with the walk.

Harry's quote above speaks to me in this instance with Mirage. She is simply one of the most difficult horses I've dealt with due to her strong mindedness. I'm grateful The Spot hasn't shown up in the riding as it has in the ground work between us. Her natural curiosity and willingness to search easily could have been shut down if I had kept on battling with her in the round pen when I starting to work with her more seriously under saddle.

But by allowing her the freedom to explore and merely directing her mind from one interest to another, I made sure that her forward thoughts were a by-product of her own desires and thus weighed nothing in my hands. Soon, I simply was able to ask for a trot and it was right there for me—no ear penning or fight—just an easy transition.

When I came across Harry's quote above in my clinic journals I immediately thought about how I believe I avoided taking the search out of Mirage in the riding by trying to force my way through to a decent walk/trot transition in the round pen. I am certain Harry is correct, and since searching is such a cornerstone in the foundation of good horsemanship, we humans do well to nurture the horse's natural tendency towards it to the very best of our abilities.

CHAPTER FIVE
The Horse's Responsibility

Monday, July 26, 2010—a four-day clinic at FitzFarm in Mankato, Minnesota.

"Give a horse a reason to do it; don't do it for him," Harry said.

This quote shares another of Harry's notions that I have found to be unique to his horsemanship. Harry is talking about the horse taking responsibility for his part of the horse/human relationship. This idea is a natural extension of Harry's general approach of considering the horse's mind, thoughts, and attention in all that we do with them.

A good example to help visualize the concept Harry was speaking about is to ask a horse to step a front foot out to the side. Sounds simple, right? Let's say a rider is in the saddle, reins-in-hands. The horse is standing still. The rider extends the hand holding the right rein out to the right, thus she offers that the horse step his right front foot directly (laterally) out in that direction.

When a rider first makes this request, the horse often, rather than stepping the foot to the side, steps the foot forward. It also is common to see the hind quarters move instead of a front foot, or to have the front and back ends move at the same time (swapping ends). These responses occur because the horse's weight and posture (and mind!) are set in readiness to go forward at the first opportunity.

This means that the horse has made no plans for the possibility that he may need to move a foot sideways or backwards. These choices simply are not readily on his menu of options.

To be able to take a lateral step in the front, the horse who is on the forehand will need to rock his weight back. By rebalancing in this way, he takes more of his weight onto the hind legs thus freeing up the front end to the point that reaching out to the side with a front leg becomes physically possible. In order for the horse to willingly rock his weight back he first must disengage the thought of going forward.

Even at a standstill, horses can have it in mind to go forward when people are working with them. When this is the case, the horses only stand by pausing their forward movement temporarily rather than by truly stopping. Truly stopping in Harry's terms would mean that they "release the thought of going forward." When horses merely pause the forward, they are mentally and physically at the ready for the next thing they do to be going forward at the exclusion of all other options. This has a horse leaning forward at the ready to take that next step as soon as the human gets out of the way and stops holding him back.

So here is where the hoof hits the highway with this example and where this quote really shines.

On the one hoof, the easiest and fastest way to get a lateral right step is to first ask the horse to back up (or at least to rock his weight back) with both reins and then flow over with one rein to ask for a front foot to step out to the side. Like magic, the horse's front end frees up and he can step over fairly quickly. But what has the horse done to get this accomplished? He has done nothing more than follow directions presented on the reins in a

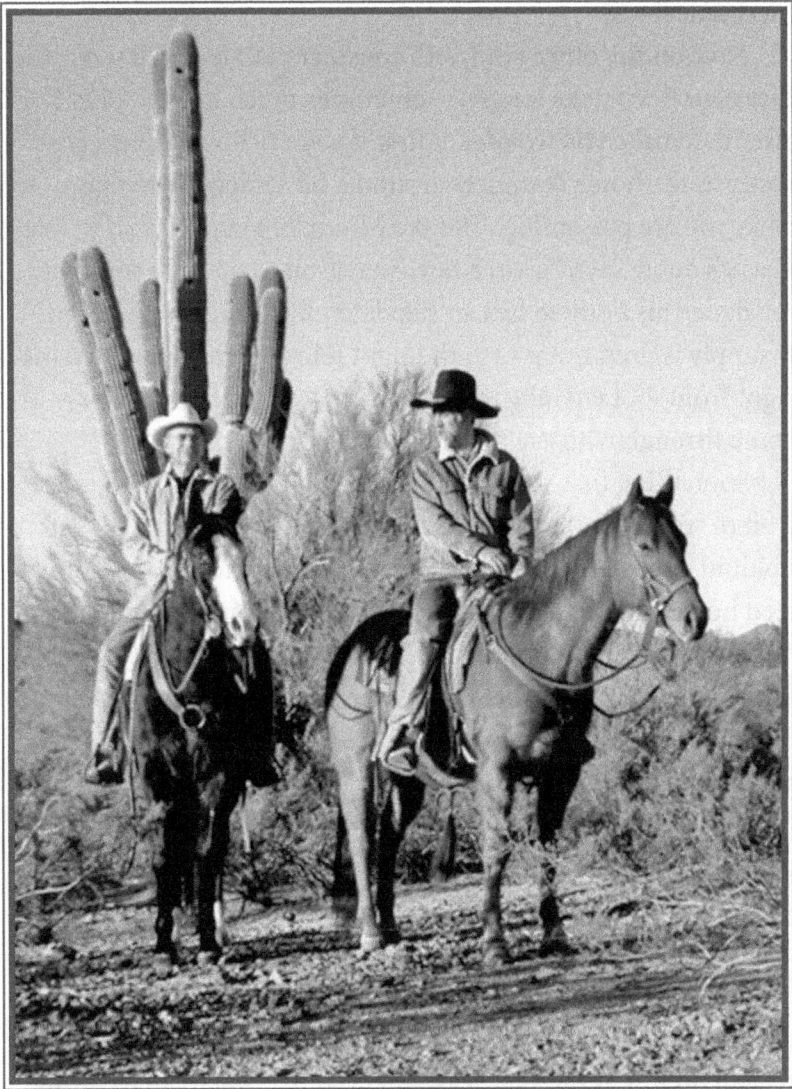

Harry and me on HZ and Beau (respectively) March 2, 2013. This photo was snapped at Harry's place in Salome, Arizona during a photo shoot for the cover of my book Going Somewhere. I love those amazing twin saguaro cacti behind us down at the far end of his arena. We were out riding early in the morning before I had to catch a plane back to Virginia with a ton of fresh notes in my clinic journal.

mechanical way.

Now on the other hoof, let's consider plan B. I will warn you that plan B will take longer—sometimes much longer. Plan B also may make you wonder at first if you are doing things correctly as the horse flounders around a bit struggling to figure out what you are presenting. But the beauty of plan B is that it, like Harry's quote says, "gives a horse a reason to do it [in this case rebalance his body so he can step laterally to the right]." Plan B simply is presenting with the right rein that the horse step his right front foot laterally to the right and waiting on the horse to come through with the move.

Something that sounds so simple in practice tends to cause a bit of trouble for folks, especially at first. One reason is that holding a rein out to the side will be a foreign feel to the uninitiated horse, although in a side-pull or snaffle bit it should amount to a somewhat directional request. It also can seem like your arm is going to fall off before he ever finds what you are asking. The horse may try to step forward, move the hind end, fling his head around, or any number of things at first to get the rider to relax the request on the rein. This is where a conversation gets going between the rider and the horse.

Harry often refers to this approach as "setting up a search" in the horse. In our example, the person asks with the right rein for the horse to step that foot to the right and hangs in there with the request until either the horse comes through with the correct answer or at the very least offers something that is "getting warmer." It also is possible that a horse might stand there completely dulled out with eyes glazed over. This would indicate a lack of searching, and the rider may need to slap her leg to make a noise, bring her energy up in her legs a little, or do something to instigate the horse to search. But once the horse is searching, the rider just holds out on the rein asking for that step in the right direction.

A reasonable scenario to expect that might unfold when trying this with a horse would be:

When the rider engages the rein, the horse immediately steps forward. The rider will not release for that since a release would tell the horse that he had the correct answer, which he does not yet. The rider may want to engage the other rein enough to block the horse's forward thought to make stepping forward not work out while continuing to offer the lateral step on the right rein.

After some frustration on the horse's part because he can't go forward as his mind insists he should, he may do something like shake his head adamantly or pull forward on the bit by poking his nose out. The rider needs to hold out through this kind of mess too, not necessarily blocking it outright with a super grip on the reins, but keeping enough pressure on the right rein so that the horse does not feel a release and keeps searching.

Perhaps next, the horse tries rocking back slightly.

Release!

That is what the rider is looking for...a "step" in the right direction. Even a good focused glance to the right would qualify as an acceptable try and should get a release in the early stages of presenting this deal.

The rider can give the horse a moment to let that success soak in and then start again. By releasing on the rein for thoughts or slight tries to the right over a number of repetitions, the horse eventually will come around and try stepping that right foot deliberately out to the side.

That's it!

The rider successfully offered a feel to the horse, blocked him from just going forward on auto pilot, and allowed him to search for what would work to return balance to the bit in his mouth and to the feel between him and the human. As always, we want the horse to understand he is in control of making imbalances between us disappear and finding a sweet spot—he just has to think about it and come up with the right answer.

With good timing and consistent releases, the horse should let go more and more of his default forward thoughts and begin to think differently. And that is the key here, that he changes his way of thinking. As he learns to try new things to sort out what the person is asking on the reins, the reins will take on new meaning.

In other words, rather than being a mechanical steering device at odds with the horse's forwardly thinking mind, the reins will begin to direct the horse's mind elsewhere. He will hear the reins and become supple of mind enough to let go of the straight ahead thinking and turn his head on the end of his neck and look to the right, for instance. When his mind becomes more directable the horse can willingly take care of moving his body along with it, and all in tune with what the rider offers.

In a herd's world where there are no humans present, it is very rare to see a horse move in a direction that he or she is not looking in. But insert a human into the equation and it is quite common to see horses looking longingly in other directions than where they are going. We can manage to add stress and anxiety to horses through our interactions with them, and it is not uncommon to see them work to get away from situations with people, at least mentally if not physically. When trying to escape mentally, their bodies belie their true desires, so things like crookedness, leaning, oblong circles, glazed over eyes, and outright fighting against the reins or lead rope become quite commonplace.

But a willingness awaits the horseperson who captures a horse's interest and develops an understanding of how to address the horse's mind. Getting horses to let go of their thoughts and search out what we are presenting is key to this with-you-ness.

The bottom line as relates to Harry's above quote really is this: if you do "it" for the horse whatever "it" is—which in this example is rebalancing his body by rocking back to be able to step a front foot over to the right side—then you always will need to do "it" for the horse. That means ten years from now, you still will be asking the horse to back with the reins before he is able to take that lateral step.

Instead, if you take the time to develop in the horse an understanding of the reins as discussed in the above example, then you need not micromanage the horse's rebalancing act. He takes care of all that within his body because he understands it is his responsibility to be prepared to step laterally if he is asked to.

A horse worked in this way may begin to stop and stand with a better balance all the time to be prepared just in case you ask him to step to the side. That becomes a distinct possibility now. Add some other things to the lateral step request we used in the example above. Try backwards, forwards, sideways, move the hind quarters, move the front quarters, or whatever you like. If the person establishes an understanding of these things with the horse through consistent requests and has insisted that he search out the right answers for himself about them, then the human may be quite amazed at just how much responsibility the horse is capable of bringing to the relationship.

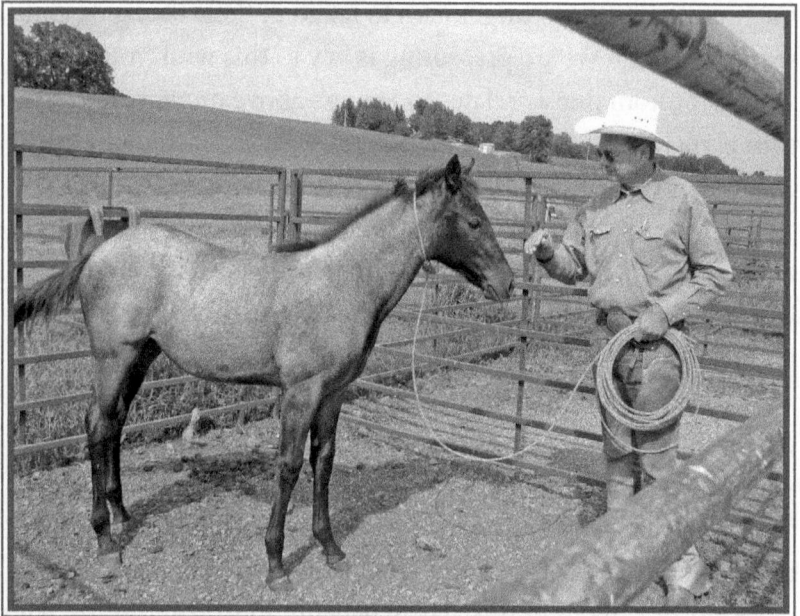

Chapter Five's quote is from a clinic held at Suzy Fitzsimmons' farm near Mankato, Minnesota. One of my favorite clinic experiences of all time happened there on that trip. It is unusual to get a chance to see Harry work with a very young horse, but Melissa Hanson brought Olive, a filly only a few months old and who was pretty much unhandled. The opportunity to see Harry put the first moments of training on a foal, well, that was exceptional! The whole clinic experience with Olive is covered in detail in Chapter Six of my book Further Along the Trail.

This photo is of Olive and Harry on July 21, 2010 as he has the filly newly okay with the lariat around her neck. She is beginning to understand and follow the feel that Harry presents. Harry began from scratch with the filly on the first day but soon after this photo was taken, Harry had Olive willingly placing her head in the halter and not long after, he was leading her all over Fitz Farm.

CHAPTER SIX

Jubal!

Thursday, June 24, 2010— Mendin' Fences Farm,
Rogersville, Tennessee.

*"If he can do that, then there's no excuse for him not to do
that,"* Harry said, speaking about Jubal's stop.

Jubal (my big, sorrel Quarter Horse who has been the
subject of many chapters in my books over the years and is often
referred to as "Jubaaal!" or "Jubal The Wonder Horse!") spent
the 2010 run of clinics at Mendin' Fences Farm in Rogersville,
Tennessee, working as Harry's saddle horse.

This chapter's quote came from a day at the end of Harry's
stay in Tennessee that year, so he and Jubal had been working
other horses together for many weeks. Riding Jubal to work
other horses of course meant that Harry had the double task
of working on Jubal so the gelding would be "with him" to the
point that he could get work done with the other horses. Harry
made the above remark in reference to Jubal's stop, or rather the
lack thereof, during a session.

The comment pointed out that the big gelding was fully
capable of stopping. So, when Harry asked for a decent stop
and did not get it, the lack of stop was in no way the result of an
inherent inability in Jubal. Therefore, other influences had to be

causing Jubal's lack of stoppage.

The above quote really is a key to many problems that occur between people and horses. Horses often prove that when they are not around us humans, they are fully capable of stopping, turning, loping, relaxing...but why then can it be the case that these desirable actions do not occur, or occur readily, or shape up as nicely, when we ask for them?

The language of Harry's quote really answers the question—"there's no excuse for him not to do that." Sounds pretty simple, right? Well, that's both the beauty and the bother of the thing....

It is simple. Horses are capable of whatever tasks. We watch them perform athletic, majestic moves in the pasture playing with the herd. Then we get them saddled, climb aboard, ask for the very same movements and, yuck! So, Harry's point indicates that it is up to us not to settle for less than what our horses are capable of when we ask for something.

It also is complicated. If all we have to do is insist that they give us what we are looking for, then wouldn't every horse and rider be top-notch? Why then is there a break down between what we want and what horses give us?

I'm still working on a wide range of things with Jubal—some are still quite basic. Is he capable of more than what I get? Certainly. But when a human gets involved, things can get sideways with him. When I ride him, he does not typically give the wonderful results he would in the pasture when full of himself and away from people. This isn't to say he doesn't have poor-looking moments out in the field with his horse companions once in awhile—he does. But it is the human interactions that predictably cause him to perform less than ideally on a regular basis.

Jubal came to me as a project packing plenty of experience with humans of the kind I'd like to erase from his memory. With

Jubal, however, I have a unique benefit in that Harry worked with him during that run of clinics in 2010.

One reason I like to ride Jubal (aside from the fact that he is majorly awesome) is because sometimes as I experiment on asking for softness, responsiveness, relaxation, and so forth in the various things that we do, when I get something right he hits a really nice spot in part because Harry worked on that with him previously. He knows from his Mendin' Fences experiences that some of these things can work in a positive way between horse and rider. That works as an educational tool. It seems to provide a way for me to have a little feedback from Jubal that might not be available to the same extent if I were working a horse whose entire training and human experiences were not as great.

In other words, I could get some of these things working with a random horse if I am handy enough and he comes through. But with Jubal, Harry established them previously. So, I am helping him re-find them; thus Jubal's memory more readily provides the feedback I can use to know if I've got something right or not. At least it feels that way to me when I get something like a half-halt, for instance, and he is right there for me and it clicks just so sweetly.

I didn't establish that with him, so it comes together rather suddenly when I ask in a "correct" way. Jubal is helping me discover just how to present some things to a horse to be effective. I may have a good idea of what needs to take place intellectually, but doing it and having a horse respond positively is a whole other deal. In that way, Jubal is proving a brilliant teacher.

It makes me a believer that this kind of thing can be a benefit for folks whose horses come through Harry's intensive clinics. The four full days Harry rides those horses is enough time to see some pretty profound changes in them. The riders who pay attention and work towards getting and maintaining those positive changes when they ride have the opportunity to feel the horses hit the sweet spots that they developed under Harry's careful guidance.

But really in all cases, we are not teaching the horse to do anything he doesn't already do and probably do much better without human help, when we work on these things. It is the horse who is showing us by how well he goes when we get our requests right (or visa versa) on how to better present what we'd like for him to do.

So, back to the quote, "*If he can do that, then there's no excuse for him not to do that.*" It says there is no excuse for the horse not to do whatever it is that we know he can do. Maybe there is no excuse, but clearly there are reasons why the horse isn't doing those things we desire when we are involved. Those reasons might include tension, worry, environmental influences (like that horse-eating chickadee in the bushes), and so on. But, all of these bring us back to one central reason for our equine dilemma—(you guessed it) the horse's mind is not on the task at hand. If the horse is to let go of whatever thoughts are in the way of him performing the task, and performing it well, then he would be available to think along with us and do it.

In the round pen that day in 2010, Jubal did not stop when Harry asked, even though he had the capacity to, because he was not thinking about stopping. I can't say what Jubal was otherwise focused on. I can tell you that he was on the forehand and plowed right on past Harry's request to stop...and since they were working another horse together, that stop would have been pretty darn important to the job right about then.

Harry often says that horses are not feeling their best unless they are performing their best. I think about that here because Jubal was not performing his best in this example. Something

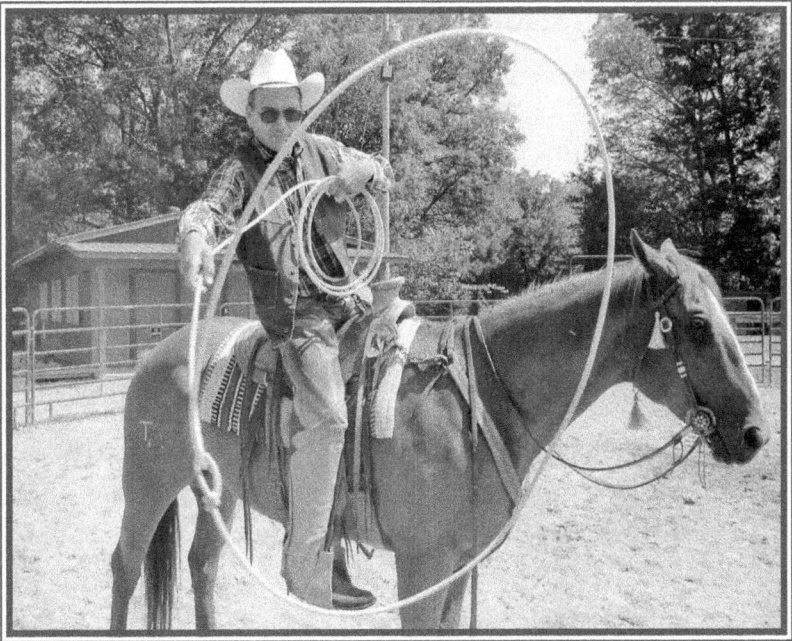

Jubal and Harry in the round pen during the 2010 run of clinics at Mendin' Fences Farm in Rogersville, Tennessee.

as simple as a botched stop indicates that the horse is not with the rider. If his mind is not on task then he likely isn't prepared in his body to do the next thing we may ask, and there is a disconnect between the two. Most of the time, that also is a reason for the horse to feel tension and tightness on whatever level. If the rider can get the horse following willingly, then the horse will soften—he will feel better, which links directly to his performing better.

Harry stopped working the other horse to focus on Jubal right then, which is what prompted him to speak to us observers and provide this chapter's quote. He asked Jubal to go... "Go!" and he got big enough to get a forward thought and then released his ask as they went forward together. He followed that by asking Jubal to stop.

Jubal again didn't do a great job of hearing Harry's request to stop, so the gelding ran into the bit and the signals sent from Harry's body offering that he stop. Harry's request escalated from asking for a stop to asking for a reverse as well. Harry was doing what was necessary to get Jubal to let go of his overwhelming forward thought. Harry did not consider Jubal's stop a true stop until he had disengaged his thought of going forward. Even if Jubal's feet had stopped (which they hadn't), Harry wouldn't have settled for it if the gelding's mind had not let go of the thought of going forward—it was a mental right-there-ness Harry sought in the gelding.

As I write this, again I wonder, "Is this simple or complicated?"

"Yes, it is!" I answer myself.

It really is not difficult to consider these things as we sit here and discuss it in a few paragraphs, but how about sitting on Jubal and getting that done? This is where I find that auditing Harry's clinics is so helpful. After watching Harry ride horses for several days straight, the onlooker can begin to see and assimilate some of the feel and timing that the clinician talks about and demonstrates during a clinic.

Especially at first, I found it was quite a bit easier to see when a horse was not thinking along with the rider when observed from a distance than it was to feel it from the saddle—a horse's eyes were not looking where the rider wanted to go, a tail swished nervously, a neck was held high, etc. From the saddle, one may not be able to see these things quite as easily. One must instead begin to get the feel and perspective of what it is like to have the horse more or less mentally with her or him while being above him on his back, and behind his head where the visuals are not so easily accessible.

Another dilemma I had at first when considering this quote was what seemed like a contradiction. To hear the words, "there's no excuse for him not to do that," gives the impression that one ought to simply not take no for an answer and force the issue.

Yes, Harry is saying don't take no for an answer. But, at the same time he is not saying we should force the outcome. That may be a bit tough to differentiate at first.

I've heard Harry say to be persistent, not insistent. Persistence goes hand-in-hoof with consistency—such as, consistently be persistent enough when you begin asking a horse to do something that you do not tolerate the horse ignoring you; consistently get big enough to reach the point that the horse searches and lets go of thoughts that get in the way of following what is being suggested by you.

Insistency by contrast would be a strong-armed, mechanical, physically forceful form of horsemanship, one where the horse's options are so limited that he feels forced to do things. Unfortunately, that kind of approach has been the mainstay of many equestrian training traditions over the years and is not what Harry means in this instance.

Being absolutely consistent and not allowing those side-tracked thoughts to work out for the horse is key. Instead, not taking no for an answer means getting big enough with what you do to get the search going in the horse so that he achieves a letting go of whatever mental side-track he is on.

Then, continue to encourage him with the feel you present to find the desirable thing it is that you want him to do. Finally, when the horse begins to come along with the right idea, be sure to build relaxation and willingness into the mix. That is

Jubal and me October 7, 2019 in Floyd, Virginia.

accomplished in part by holding the releases to the point that you convince the horse not just to perform a task, but you encourage him more and more to perform whatever it is in a manner he would if he were out in the pasture with the desire to do it himself—as if it was his own idea.

To provide a little more context for this quote, I'll share the note that follows it in my clinic journal showing what Harry said next: "*All it takes is one time in 42 for the horse to think something might work better for him; he'll work 41 times harder then to try for that.*"

This makes me think about the difference between working a Jubal, who brings to the round pen a ton of experience with humans and "training," and is in many ways not the better for it, and working with a horse who lacks such experiences, like the colts in Harry's colt starting clinic back in 2014 that are discussed in great detail in my book trilogy, *Six Colts, Two Weeks*, and who do not have such a tangled mental web of bad (or at the very least, unhelpful) experiences with people that needs to be unraveled.

While the points that Harry made mentioned above are true for horses in general, colts like those in that colt starting clinic have not yet had the chance to experience those "one time in 42" moments as Jubal has. It makes me wonder about the prospects of a perfect scenario. One where, say, a person had a young horse and every single time the person asked for the colt to let go of a thought and go along with another one, the timing and feel were handled well. And this went on from the very beginning and always throughout the horse's life. That horse potentially would present the closest possible example of doing something at the human's suggestion that was of a spontaneous nature like that of his own pure variety as we see out in the human-less herd.

The point of thinking about that kind of thing for me is in part an exercise in following Harry's statements to their fullest extent...to think of their truths taken to their ultimate forms. Of course, no one can be so consistent as in my mental exercise. But it still seems very reasonable to me that if people thought about the potential that is there in a horse—that they notice how a horse stops in the field when the desire to do so comes from within himself, for example—that the motivation to get horses feeling and performing as close to that ideal as possible when we interact with them should move us to improve our horsemanship to that end.

It certainly does for me!

CHAPTER SEVEN
Who's Driving the Bus?

Wednesday, June 18, 2014— Mendin' Fences Farm, Rogersville, Tennessee.

"Our horses should be busy keeping up with what we're doing—not the other way around—and not so busy that it's troubling to the horse," Harry said.

Many excellent examples of what Harry was getting at in this quote have shown up during the horsemanship lessons and clinics that I have taught over the years. Indeed, I recognized what he was saying and jotted it down because it is something that I realized I can be guilty of and need to keep in mind to avoid.

One place where I often see instances of this flip-flopping of roles is during groundwork when a person asks a horse to walk around him or her on line in a circle. Looking at some aspects of circling a horse can demonstrate both sides of the quandary that Harry presented in the quote above.

To begin, let me discuss how one can get a horse to "keep up with what we're doing."

A typical scenario starts with the person standing with the horse facing her. Next, she must offer a feel on the lead rope for the horse to step his front end over to a side before starting to walk the circle around her. This initial step, however, can require a concentrated effort for people to get shaped up. One common reason it can be tricky is because of the natural tendency for folks to want to pull a horse forward with the lead rope. People have a hard time believing that a horse can follow a feel presented on a slack lead rope. It seems they believe they must offer a pull to get the horse moving.

When a person feels the need to pull a horse forward to begin the circling, the person often sticks her arm straight out to her side to indicate the direction for the horse to circle. Then, she takes the slack out of the rope. Next, she pulls the rope to get the horse to go forward. This arrangement causes the horse to follow exactly what is being presented, which is to come straight forward along the path of the tight rope which is in her hand, an arm's length off to her side. The horse, being the large creature

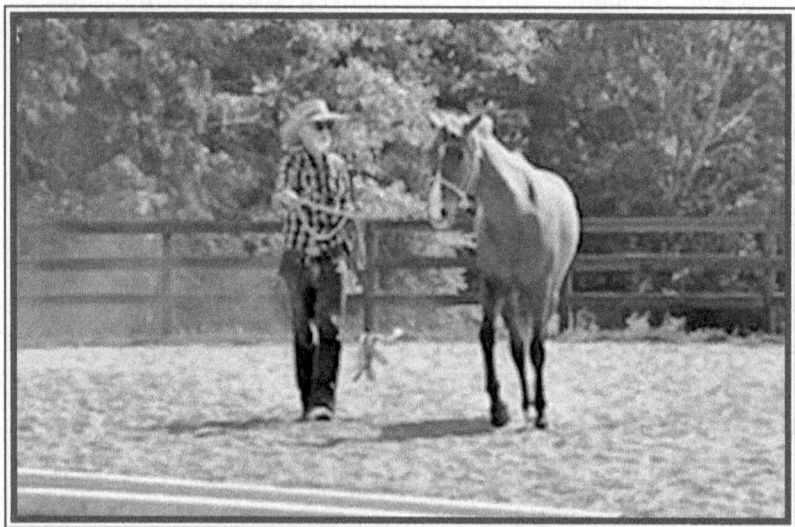

Newly (my new two-year-old) and me working on circling on line during the second week of our annual Bible/horsemanship clinic on August 22, 2023 in Floyd, Virginia. (Photo: Jaime McArdle)

that he is, finds himself on a forward trajectory where he walks too close to his person, maybe even bumping into her.

Instead of letting this scenario go unchecked if this happens in a lesson or clinic, I like to coach a person to offer a feel along a slack lead rope. I work to get her to ask the horse to take a strong look in the direction of the upcoming circle, and then to take lateral steps with the front end in that direction while pivoting on the hind end.

Harry teaches the importance of getting a horse's thought to lead in this situation—to take a good look where we want him to go first—and then to let the horse carry himself as directed. Getting that intent look from the horse before getting a step is a good indication that his thoughts are on-board with the feel we are presenting, and soon his body can be there too.

The horse must rock his weight back (rebalance, or have been in a very balanced position initially) to accomplish this. When a horse rocks back and steps his front end over while pivoting on the hind end, he then can get his body onto the correct orbit of the circle we seek with all four feet. Once the horse has stepped the front end over, simply stepping forward puts him in the right position to be "out there" circling the person.

So that stage of setting a horse up to circle often gets sorted out first, which provides a nice example of how to present a feel for a horse to follow so he can "keep up with what we're doing," to quote this chapter's quote.

And that brings us to the circling part. What I often see next is that the person loses the lead role and begins to follow the horse. Sometimes, a person even stops offering anything whatever to the horse and just stands there sort of stiff and lifeless. She expects the horse to circle her mostly motionless body with only her arms switching the rope around her to keep from being wrapped up like a mummy.

In the groundwork, as is likewise true in the riding, the person has the opportunity to offer something for the horse to follow. In the example here, let's say the person wants a basic walk. To achieve this, the person needs to have the idea of that walk in her head—the speed, the direction, and the distance out from her that the horse will walk. Then, she must present that walk to the horse. She also needs to be prepared to make things not work out so well if the horse has other ideas so the horse can search and find what is being offered by the human.

The key is to have the horse's thought focused on what the person presents and to develop the willingness to follow along with the person. That is a broad statement, but let's consider here what the circling might look like.

In our circling at a walk example, the ideal set-up will look something like this: the person has asked the horse to step over on the circle and begin walking as discussed above. The person is walking at the rate she wants the horse to walk. The person is lined up facing a side of the horse so that from her nose to her toes she is sending her feel towards the horse to roughly the shoulder/base of the neck area. She is presenting a feel along the lead rope by holding out a hand in the direction of the circle with slack floating in the line between her and the horse. And, she is walking her own little circle inside of the horse's bigger circle, both of which synch up (think of a point on an axle spinning to a corresponding point out on a wheel).

The horse will have a bend through his whole body following the arc of the circle that he is walking. His neck and head will be extending out from his body without being elevated. His face will be plumb, and he will be stepping equally with all four legs in a balanced way that matches the effort being presented by the person as he takes his body along with his forward thought on the circle the person is presenting. So those are qualities we'd like to see when the person is offering a nice circling walk to the horse and the equine is attentive and willing.

But so often at this stage, rather than the horse keeping up with what the person is doing, as Harry's quote suggests, it happens the other way around.

This can manifest and be seen in lots of ways. Sometimes it is as simple as the person turning and walking parallel to the horse where her position is not particularly poor, but her feet and body are turned away from the horse and she is stepping beside and in the same direction as him. In this case, the human's energy (feel, or whatever we might call that link we establish with the horse) has been shifted away from being pointed at the horse's shoulder/base of the neck and is shooting out in front of the horse somewhere. The person no longer is presenting a walk to the horse but is stepping in time to what the horse is doing in a parallel but mostly separate universe.

Another way to see the person following the horse's lead is when a person lags behind the horse's body. Sometimes a person will be stepping towards the hind quarters. This can be the residuals of a person who has been in the habit of driving a horse forward rather than offering a feel for the horse to go with. The horse can take the notion that the person is driving him forward, or sometimes the horse is going at the pace he prefers and the person is just tagging along but in no way leading the operation.

It really isn't hard to see these kinds of things, and it is quite observable when the horse is initiating the speed and/or direction rather than the other way around. I find that I can sort of feel the difference when watching someone circle a horse. If the person is busy keeping up with the horse one can feel a passive attitude in the person and a more bold feel coming from the horse. Also, there are questions that can help detect this. Is the horse's attention on the person? Is there a horse's ear dialed onto the human? Is the horse's body relaxed or is there tension evident in rigidity, a high head, or other less desirable postures? When a horse is willingly following a person, a relaxation enters the equation, while a more tense horse is less likely to have his mind fully on and listening to the person.

As I consider all this, an odd conclusion comes to mind: there can be a number of reasons why this happens...and yet there really is only one reason why this happens.

The possible reasons include the horse taking over because he notices a lack of capable leadership coming from the human. I love an analogy of Harry's about this—he says to imagine you are on a bus flying down the freeway and you look over and the driver's seat is empty. What do you do? You go get in the driver's seat and start driving the bus, right? That's exactly what a horse does, and how the horse may feel about being dropped by the human.

Another possible reason can be a horse switching to auto-pilot. If a horse has been longed excessively in the past, for instance, he knows the routine and may think it is time to go trot circles mindlessly around the person when asked to circle her. And, that's exactly what he does with no consideration for what input the human is attempting to offer.

In another possible scenario, a horse may be worried about his buddies over in the barn and the anxiety causes him to speed up and be counter-bent on the circle rather than give the nice, relaxed, easy walk the person is presenting.

Those all are possible, but there really is only one reason this kind of thing happens, and that is that people allow it to happen.

Okay, you can argue that a horse with severe mental issues may be impossible to get to follow along with the human, but we're not talking about a horse that would by some serious defect not be a candidate for any real relationship with a person. We are talking about the vast majority of horses that people are working with.

If we look once again at Harry's quote, "*Our horses should be busy keeping up with what we're doing—not the other way around—and not so busy that it's troubling to the horse*," the reason people fail to get horses busy keeping up with what they are doing is that people fail to get big enough to get their minds centered on the business at-hand.

We end up again at the very foundation of the best kind of horsemanship, that which asks the horse to focus here, now, because there is something important to do, to trust us, and to follow along with what we offer.

It is simple in a way, but to achieve it requires certain things of us people. We must be reliable and consistent. We must determine the proper timing for setting up searches with horses, and for releases. And, as the last part of that quote stresses, "not [be] so busy that it's troubling to the horse."

This last bit really brings home to me how much of a moving target this quote speaks to. I think of how different each horse is. What is troubling to my horse Jubal may be nowhere near what it takes to trouble Mirage, my mare who spooks at practically nothing and lets things go easily. Getting busy with a really quick minded horse may help engage his mind and settle him. But a slower processing horse may be easily worried if too much action is asked of him too quickly—and so forth.

In the end, I think Harry's quote is very helpful for reminding me that it is my responsibility to keep on-task with my horses...to provide them with dependable tasks to follow and that I not be lulled into following along with them instead, making them feel the need to drive the bus. With some horses, that can mean riding every single step, at least for some time. With other horses, well, you can have them following along much more easily and without nearly that much adult supervision. And that I must not be complacent and think that one approach fits all horses—I must dial in the jobs I do with different horses to fit their individual needs.

Another thing that Harry says that kind of wraps up this discussion for me is this (I'm paraphrasing): all horses are born with the desire to follow a capable leader, but in the absence of that capable leader they take control of the situation and look out for their own well-being.

So the big question becomes, what is a "capable leader" to any given horse? It will be very different for a strong-minded mare than for an easy-going gelding, but either way I need to be driving the bus. If I slip out of the driver's seat into a passenger's seat and nobody is driving the bus that's barreling down the freeway, then the horse is going to jump into that seat and start driving...and I can't blame him for that; he should!

CHAPTER EIGHT
A Proper Fit

Wednesday, May 25, 2011— Mendin' Fences Farm, Rogersville, Tennessee.

"Let her think she's training you not to have a fit," Harry remarked.

Developing the skill of pitching a proper fit is a brilliant bit of horsemanship finesse helpful in achieving the higher tiers of communication with horses. I realized this fact early on in my studies with Harry, and it has been confirmed by my own experiences many times over the years.

It sounds comical, I know, but it is true.

The preceding chapters illuminate in various ways how true communication and improved relationships between horses and humans stem from working with horses' minds. The way to go about accessing horses' thoughts is to capture their attention. One good way to do that, in all honesty, is to have a well-timed fit.

The irony is that a human having a fit seems like a good way to worry the horse and drive the flee-from-fear animal away. Certainly it can be. A person acting like a fool, giving mixed messages, or seeming to be aggressive, can be deeply troubling to a horse. But the dubious nature of the horse, who is typically on the lookout for things to flee from, is what makes a fit a real attention-getter. The timing of the fit is what makes it either a negative experience or a positive tool for gaining a horse's focus and motivates him to leave whatever side-tracked thought he may have at one moment and begin to search out and try other things the next.

A key to this helpful approach is touched on in this chapter's Harry quote—"*Let her think she's training you not to have a fit.*"

Immediately, several important things jump out at me about this statement.

First, Harry was referring to a horse thinking ("let her think," he said). He was suggesting to the person he spoke to in that clinic that she needed to address and engage the horse's mind. The owner needed the mare to think, and think something specific.

To confuse things right away in an attempt to be accurate, I should say that humans can not make horses have a (specific) thought. This is a point I've heard Harry discuss many times over the years. Perhaps the best way to explain this idea is with an example.

Say, for instance, we are leading a horse with a halter and lead rope and we want him to go ahead of us through a gate. We do not have the ability to put the thought of going through that gate directly into his mind. What we can do is influence the horse to begin to search out options and think about trying something different from what he is doing at the moment.

Perhaps the horse in our example only recently has been introduced to leading and is doing quite well. But he has never been asked to go ahead of a person through an open gate before. I can lead him over to the open gate and put myself in a good position to offer with a feel on the rope that he step past me and go through the gate. At first, however, our example horse has no idea what is being asked of him.

If I were just to stand there not asking anything of the horse but maintaining a good feel between us, if his mind isn't bothered or busy, he likely will just stand there with me (fully aware of me) contented. That's a neutral spot where there is a good feel established between us and the world is rosy.

Next, I put a feel on the lead rope which to me signals that he should step forward through the gate. In our example, he has no idea what that means because it is new to him. My ask (sending a feel along the lead rope in this case) creates an "imbalance" between us. I'd like for him to start to try something, that he would react to that imbalance by doing this or that to see if he can find something that gets a "release" from me and gets us back to that neutral sweet spot.

The trial and error involved in this process shows what I meant by saying that I can not put a thought in his head. Even if I get lucky and he chooses going through the gate immediately on the first try, it doesn't change that I did not make him have that thought. Rather, I changed things between us so that standing there contentedly no longer was working out. If he first tried some other action I was not looking for, I would make that not work out so well either. I would keep on offering the imbalance until he struck upon the idea that works out best for him and returns things between us to a neutral sweet spot again.

Stated differently, I am unable to make him immediately just think to go through the gate. When I offer that he do so, he very well may back up, push a shoulder into me, or step away from me. What I can do is have him be attentive to me and begin to offer different tries like these in an attempt to get rid of the imbalance I am presenting. Then, and this is the big moment, when he comes up with the idea that I was looking for *on his own*, I release and we experience that neutral sweet spot together again.

Sometimes, however, what happens is that the horse mentally goes elsewhere and rather than seeking to come into harmony with the human, he displaces his attention away from the person. This can be seen in a horse looking away from a person and perhaps trying to escape in that direction, putting his head down low to sniff the ground, glazing over as he withdraws into his own la-la-land, or exhibiting other behaviors that are not really searches but show that he is avoiding being attentive to us. Those kinds of things are instead attempts to mentally (and perhaps physically) get away from us altogether.

I want to add a little rabbit trail to the discussion here that relates somewhat to the topic that we are kicking around. That is to point out one major reason why I think that using treats to train horses is not desirable. If a person were to use a treat in this example to bait the horse to pass through the gate (or for any other reason, like going into a trailer), the person has not really gotten the horse to have the thought of going through the gate. The horse had the thought of going to get to the treat. That is not the same thing and is not building a relationship with the horse as a willing partner who readily follows what we present because we have established understanding and trust. We have merely established that we are the keepers of the treats and can thus manipulate the horse with them.

The second thing that jumps out at me about Harry's quote is the idea it presents that humans can get horses to think that they are training us. I mentioned timing above, and this is where that aspect of the equation really comes into play. How do horses learn what works and what doesn't with each other or with people?

As we've been discussing, some "imbalance" enters into the situation. Horses prefer that things be neutral (relaxed, okay, in synch, etc.) in their worlds. When horses are not at neutral with others (people or horses) in their immediate surroundings, they typically search for an answer that equalizes relationships and restores things in their environment back to a happy neutral. That all sounds a bit academic, but I hope it conveys the idea.

With proper timing, a horse can be made to understand that she is in control of restoring her world to that balanced state. I think it is her perception of being in control that gives truth to Harry's statement that a horse can feel as though she is training the person. To follow our example, let's say I go from standing by the open gate in an at-ease fashion to offering with a feel on the rope that the horse walk through. That offer creates the kind of imbalance I have been talking about until she then starts to try to find a way to get back to neutral.

She may try moving one way or the other to see if that helps get rid of the "pressure." When she steps through the gate, or at least steps in the right direction at first, I will release my "ask" and the imbalance coming from me disappears. Thus, she has begun to figure out that she has it in her ability to search out an answer that restores a pleasant neutral to her world. That can begin to encourage a great deal of confidence in a horse since rather than feeling like she is a victim of circumstances, where things are being done to her and she must panic or simply react, she begins to understand. She realizes that when dealing with me when something becomes out of kilter, she can engage her mind, think through it, and that there is an answer that she can provide to make everything okay. She learns, in essence, that she can train me to relax my ask on the lead rope by going through the gate.

And then there is the third thing, which brings us back to the fit.

It might seem odd at first for a horsemanship clinician to

encourage someone to have a fit around her horse. But, when one spends a little time with Harry one comes to understand that the fit is very useful when a horse's mind is distracted. Since we need the horse's mind to be centered with us to have a relaxed and willing horse as we discussed in earlier chapters, we must find effective ways to gain the horse's attention. A fit certainly can help accomplish this task.

The instance at the clinic Harry was referring to with his quote was one where the fit was particularly helpful. He was speaking about a horse being so far gone mentally that she was unable to hear the owner's request on the lead rope. The mare was in the habit of taking her thoughts away from the person. This showed by the horse having a high head position, plenty of tight muscles indicative of anxiety, and the prancing desire to get her body out of the pen and over to where her thoughts really were at that time.

Harry encouraged the owner to have a fit. I have heard Harry help people develop their fits many times. It can be very difficult for the meek to bring up even a little fit, and it can be equally challenging to keep the more gregarious in check with the intensity of their fits. Harry suggests many options for a proper fit: stomping, kicking dirt, making noises, slapping chaps or the ground with the end of a lead rope, cartwheels (which I have witnessed on more than one occasion), and back-flips (which to my knowledge he has yet to instigate, but I'm still hoping to see at a clinic sometime). The point being, a fit is, well...a fit—something out of the ordinary and big enough to make an impression on a horse who is ignoring a person.

It did not require a fit of much effort to startle the horse in this instance, a mere hop/stomp combo. When a horse lets go of her side-tracked thoughts and comes to check in with the person, that is the moment to quit the fit. A quick fit was all it took with the sensitive mare at the clinic. At other times, a person may need to sustain or even intensify a fit to break through the mental road block in the way of accessing a horse's mind.

The startle the mare displayed at the clinic did not come from the owner being overly aggressive when presenting her fit, but rather it resulted from the fit interrupting the mare's errant thoughts. That kind of interruption does more to cause a horse to recoil than does the fact that some energy was expended by a person in the vicinity in some silly display of behavior. If you pitched the very same fit beside the horse when her mind was already focused on you, chances are there would be much less or no recoil at all, merely a look of concern for your sanity, if that.

At the clinic when the horse was mentally present there for just a moment post-fit, she let down an ounce after her reaction to being "startled." Then she went back to her routine of being mentally distracted again. Harry coached the owner to have another fit with a well-timed release. The result was the same.

To make the long story short, with Harry's coaching the owner timed her fits to occur just as the horse's mind became committed to going away from her. That consistent interruption provided the understanding in the horse that as long as she did not lose track of the person mentally, no fits happened. If the mare let her mind wander, she began to understand that the person got stupid as a result, which was unsettling to her. Therefore, even though the person initiated this situation, it had a predictable outcome. It was set up in such a way that the mare could think that she was training the owner not to have a fit by remaining attentive.

To relate this back to our example, the fit would occur when I went to ask the horse to go through the open gate and she was not even mentally present to hear my request. A well timed fit would act as a means to bring back the horse's attention so we then could work on having her hear and understand my request to step through the gate.

Strange though it may seem at first, the fit is an important tool in the horseman's toolbox. Without the horse's focus we have no way to bring about understanding and willingness with our equine partner. I had not been to too many Harry Whitney clinics before I found it wise to keep a fit in my horsemanship kit right beside some other skills with more highly regarded reputations.

CHAPTER NINE
Wallowing Around

Monday, March 27, 2006—Harry's place, Salome, Arizona.

"Don't let her just wallow around out there," Harry said.

We are going way back for this one to where it all began for me—back to my very first Harry Whitney horsemanship clinic experience. This quote is from the journal I kept during the trip I made out to Arizona to meet Harry for the first time in early 2006.

I have shared quite a bit about this trip in my Honest Horsemanship series of books, so I won't rehash that again here. Suffice it to say that I stayed at Harry's for two life-changing weeks of clinics on that trip, and things have never been the same since! This quote comes from the first day of the second week of clinic.

The notes I jotted down directly after this quote add insight and begin to address the idea Harry was getting at when he spoke those words:

"The statement clearly shows that it is Harry's belief that it is our responsibility to not let the horse get lost when we are together. 'Wallowing around' means mentally even more than physically

because if she wasn't lost mentally, you would never see her lost in her movements. And, thus, we have it within our power to keep our horses clearly guided and do it in such a way that they are happy inside, both from clear communication and because it is presented in such a way that the horse feels she has made the choice to be there."

There is quite a bit in all this to chew on, but I'll start by saying that I remember the horse, the person, and the moment that Harry was referring to. He used the term "wallowing" for a good reason. The mare was showing in a big way that she was uncertain about what was being asked of her and she lacked focus. She side-stepped, jigged, and seemed to throw out every simple move she had except, ironically, what the person thought he was asking her to do in the first place.

She was not trying to leave physically in a big way, i.e. in a panic, hitting the end of the lead rope, or other dust-flying kinds of movements. It was rather a squirmy deal brought on by a lack of clarity and, it seemed to me, trust in and/or consideration for the person.

In those follow-up notes above I began by saying, "The statement clearly shows that it is Harry's belief that it is our responsibility to not let the horse get lost when we are together." That statement refers to the part of the quote where Harry says, "*don't allow* her to...." With those words he puts the responsibility to keep the horse from wallowing on us humans. So, how exactly do you not allow a horse to go wallow around?

The answer to that question is found in the same place as are many of the other spots we have discussed so far—namely, getting big enough to get a change in the horse's attention and thinking, and to be consistent with how we handle our asks and releases.

That is a simplification to be sure, but it is accurate.

In the clinic, the fellow ended up getting some nice changes that settled the horse and had her following along with his requests much better. To be honest, I was mesmerized by Harry's ways. I had never seen anything quite like this before my trip to Arizona, and I had been looking obsessively for answers about how to get better with horses. It seemed like Harry could read horses' minds—he knew what was going on with these amazing creatures on a level that was uncanny. After watching this session, and many of the others during that trip, it was becoming clear to me that a person truly has the opportunity to not only communicate well with a horse, but to bring about a relaxed and better feeling in the horse as a result of doing it.

From a vantage point by the panels at the round pen, I could easily see at first that the fellow was too wishy-washy with the requests he made of his horse during the groundwork to be clear about what he wanted. A change came when Harry coached him into having a better picture in mind of what he wanted the horse to do, and by being more definite and assertive in how he asked for it. Immediately, the mare shaped up quite a bit. It was as if she had been longing for someone to step in and let her know what to do. She was not a rogue, difficult horse in any way but rather a pretty sweet mare. He needed only a couple of ounces of firm decisiveness to get her much more attentive and willing to his requests.

Then, a repetition of more assertive requests made a huge improvement in how the mare backed, stepped here or there, stopped, and went to circle around him. The mare began to keep a watchful eye on him and settled down in general. That attentiveness was a part of fixing the wallowing issue. Another part was that the owner now had a better idea in mind what he was asking and how he was going to go about it. Plus, he was being big enough to convince the horse to try and search out what was being asked. The sweet spot between them already was part of their relationship, so releases did not seem to be a problem.

The lesson proved to me that a person can and should take responsibility to provide what a horse needs so she need not experience uncertainty. Uncertainty is not a horse's friend and will cause her all kinds of bothers, including feeling the need to wallow around.

I think about the overt example of wallowing that was provided to me that day and it leads me to consider less obvious ones, too. In my notes I mention that Harry's use of the term "wallowing" was more of a mental reference than a physical one. My thought was that if you see wallowing, then the horse first must have been mentally wallowing to produce it. Taken a step further, I believe there are instances where a horse wallows in her head but shows it much less in her actions than in the above example—but it is still the same thing.

Jubal can provide an example of what I mean. I've been riding him a lot this winter. One of the things I have been focusing on is how he gets crooked in his body when we are riding somewhere that is at a distance from the other horses, and especially when traveling in a direction away from them. Crookedness can be a form of wallowing.

I think of it this way—a horse who is unfamiliar with letting go of his thoughts in general can get crooked in his body. If he is crooked and we pick up a rein or otherwise begin to address the crookedness, he can wallow around rather than simply think along with us and the feel we present on the rein. If the horse is not in the habit of letting go of his thoughts and we are not effective with getting through to him, picking up a rein actually can increase the tension, crookedness, and wallowing in the horse at first.

Addressing the crookedness directly is more beneficial after we have worked through this kind of thing a number of times with the horse. It is with work and time that the horse develops the understanding that we are presenting something he can go with that will allow him to let go of whatever is on his mind and find a sweet spot with us in it. This is more of a cumulative experience than some instant fix. Jubal has accumulated a whole bunch of these to get to the point where we are today.

The other day I was riding Jubal in a pasture. I asked him to walk away from Festus and Mirage who were in sight. We were two pastures and several fences away from them. Jubal stalled his walk and his head cocked off to one side on the end of his crooked neck. I began to address the crookedness.

Jubal really was wallowing around like the horse in the clinic back in Arizona even though it was presenting in much less overt ways. Wallowing has the same kind of feel coming from the horse to me regardless of how big a dose gets served up. I was riding along, Jubal was mentally seeking his buddies, and the result was that his head tipped this way or that on the end of his neck, a shoulder leaned in a little on one side, and he got a slight bend designed to leave my trajectory and aim for his.

These all manifested in very small ways, but now that I am aware of crookedness and am working on getting horses straight, these habits really stood out to me. At first when I blocked these things and asked for a change in Jubal's mindset, he did other crooked things but still did not line out and go along with what I was asking. He was wallowing around. But rather than expressed in a big wallowy way, it was in a pretty tight package and really took place mostly right between the reins.

When we were walking away from his friends, he had to pick one side or the other to focus on—whichever one he thought got him closer to turning around to go back towards his buddies. I offered a little feel on the rein opposite his mental draw to help him think about tipping his head back straight on the end of his neck. I also needed to offer a feel (this tends to be a combination of how I hold the reins and offering with a little leg) to move his shoulder over so he was straight through his whole body. All the while, I was asking him to walk on out straight and take me somewhere.

At times when we work on this, I can feel him squirm under me. But then sometimes moments occur when he just lets all that junk go and he gets lined-out through his whole body. When this happens, we walk straight on in synch together and it feels like I could ask anything of him at that moment and he would be right there for me. It is as if he becomes totally available and willing to my requests. These moments can be fleeting, but they happen more and more, and at distances further and further away from the other horses.

Enough good work has been accomplished between us now that at times a little firmness on a rein is all it takes for him to say, "Oh, right, I lost the plot," and come back to being with me. It is similar to the result of having one of those fits discussed in the previous chapter (or the positive changes the fellow got with his mare after Harry spoke this chapter's quote). But when your fit amounts to simply putting a little feel on a rein, it starts to seem like you really are getting somewhere with your horse.

***

At the risk of side-tracking a bit far from the wallowing discussion before circling back to it, I want to address another point that jumps off the page at me from my notes above. That is that we can *keep our horses clearly guided*, but the guidance must be "*presented in such a way that the horse feels she has made the choice to be there*." Can we really present requests to a horse in a way that she feels like she had a choice and came to the "right" conclusion on her own? I'm convinced the answer to that question is yes.

I think it is easier to discern how we can provide clear guidance to our horses than it is to see that we can set things up so they feel that they made a choice for themselves. This is a tricky bit to discuss, but let me begin this way—clear guidance can be observed at times, though not always.

Clear guidance can look like a person getting busy with a flag, slapping a chap, or having one of those fits when the horse's mind goes AWOL. Guidance can look like a rider holding the reins from the saddle or holding driving reins while walking behind the horse. Guidance can look like nothing more than a person standing in the center of the round pen with a horse at liberty in the pen with her. You get the point; guidance can look like anything, because it is how a person communicates a feel to a horse that counts, and there are nearly endless possibilities as to how that might work out.

The thing is, boundaries can be set by a person providing guidance to a horse all while a range of options remain available for the horse to explore within those boundaries. Even when a person asserts herself into the equation and limits some options to the horse, enough options need to remain so that the horse still feels like she had a choice to feel "happy inside" and like she "made the choice to be there," to quote my notes.

Boundaries can be as obvious as the panels of a round pen. The horse is trapped within the space of that corral, but a horse can come up with a whole slew of things to try within the space of a round pen if the person doesn't completely shut them down. A more narrow boundary set-up could be having a horse on a lead rope standing beside the open door of a trailer where she has only a few feet to move around. Still, she has a bunch of options to explore even in that scenario if the person allows a search to take place, like backing away from the trailer, smelling the trailer floor, putting one foot into the trailer, etc.

The physical space can be reduced further again, even to the point where there is practically no room for the horse to move around at all, and yet mentally a whole range of options remain open for the horse to explore with the person if allowed to do so. I am convinced that if things are handled well, a horse can search out her options in a very short time and in very tight quarters and end up feeling no different than if she spent 30 minutes exploring her options on the end of a lead rope.

Sometimes a person (like Harry) can provide clear guidance to a horse but in so slight a manner as to be indiscernible to the observer. It can transpire that all that is necessary to get a conversation accomplished between a person and a horse is a bit of feel.

That's the kind of relationship I want with my horses, where the exchange of a quick feel sorts all that stuff out. That in an eye-blink, the horse gets willing to go along with what I ask because she feels like she had choices and she picked the best one. Or perhaps that because of our established relationship, the horse knows and trusts what I have to say. She simply has confidence in me to follow along with what I'm pointing out as the best choice to begin with. The more we operate in this kind of reality, the more the horse has a chance to make letting go of her other thoughts, that aren't going to work out, a comfortable habit.

The thing that is quite observable, however, (and is a good test to know if there has been success in sorting out this kind of thing) is simply to see how the horse reacts to requests from the person. Does the horse wallow or not? If the horse willingly, relaxedly (is that a word? I guess it is now...), and deliberately undertakes an action that has been instigated by a person, then clear guidance has been a part of the equation. It stands to reason that if the horse looks that good, then she feels that good since horses really do not separate how they feel from how they act.

About a year or so before I took this first trip out to Arizona to meet Harry, I met Ray Hunt at one of his clinics. One of the most astonishing things I witnessed Ray do was to sort out what was as bad a case of wallowing as I have ever seen. How Ray did it flabbergasted me at the time. I'll never forget the profound effect it had on me as an eye-opener to what is possible when working with horses.

There was a teenage girl at Ray's clinic with a Thoroughbred that towered above her...a very tall, lean horse. The horse was tacked up in an English saddle and bridle, and the girl likewise had her English-wear on. She and the horse were in an arena with 20 other horses and riders and the clinic was underway.

The girl had a portable mounting block. I watched for at least ten minutes as she attempted to steady her wallowing horse, set the block on the ground in position to get aboard, and try to mount only to have the extremely tense horse wallow away. The girl picked up her mounting block and chased the enormous creature around, reins in one hand mounting block in the other, got the horse to stop, set the mounting block in place, only to have him prance off again. The girl's frustration was obvious, and it left me feeling sorry for the horse who, by this time, was so nervous that he was as tight as a fiddle string, sweating, and had a lather going in his mouth.

Ray had been instructing the riders to ride in two big circles around the arena, one inside of the other going in opposite directions, and then weave the horses in and out past one another. That was a colossal wreck in itself with people and horses floundering all over the place. All the while, the girl kept chasing her horse around with the mounting block at one end of the arena.

Finally, during a pause in the action Ray went over to the girl and her horse. I was standing right there on the other side of the fence when he approached them. He took a hold of the reins very close to the bit and backed that horse, getting plenty big with his ask, and got a real change of thought. The horse's head shot up and the look on his face was like, "What the heck? Who is this guy? Wow!"

Ray backed that horse until he truly backed up, which took about six feet. Then he brought him forward, backed him a second time in the same manner, brought him forward, backed him a third time where the horse backed immediately and with an effort, and then they stood there.

A few moments later while they stood there, I could see that Ray's hand was moving slightly. I am certain that he had a whole conversation with that horse with his hand moving maybe in the space of about one square inch with those reins. The horse let down, chilled out, and stood calm as could be—no more wallowing. The girl set her mounting block, and with the horse's mind centered she had no trouble stepping up and throwing a leg over the horse. He stood like a champ.

The understanding I had before that moment observing Ray and the Thoroughbred said to me that sure, a horse like that could be helped to quit wallowing and get to a better, calmer place with some groundwork. You know, some sessions of getting big with a flag, circling, that kind of thing—but, not a couple of back-and-forths and a minute of holding the reins close to the chin.

I realized then that the feel a person presents to a horse can say everything that needs to be said to gain confidence, willingness, and relaxed-ness, and it may be barely visible, or even invisible for all I know. That deal with Ray showed me what was possible, but it wasn't until I met Harry Whitney that I had any idea of why and how it was possible. And the really nice thing about all these Harry Whitney clinics I've attended and quotes I've collected from him over the years is that Harry has helped me stop wallowing around so much, too!

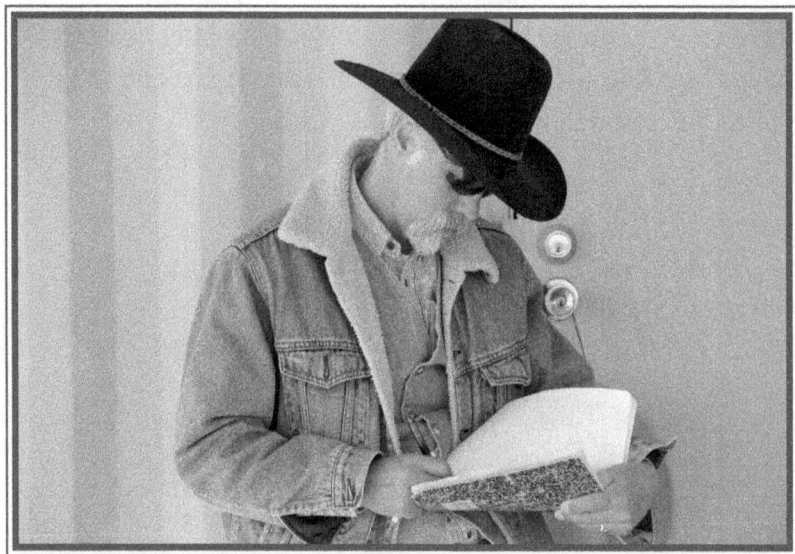

Filling yet another clinic notebook out by the round pen at Harry's place in Salome, Arizona on February 27, 2013. (Photo: Bob Grave)

CHAPTER TEN

When to Do Quite a Little

Monday, March 27, 2006—Harry's place, Salome, Arizona.

"If they're getting involved and it affects their emotions, I'm going to do quite a little," Harry explained.

Timing is an aspect of horsemanship that can be tricky to master. It also can be difficult to convey to other folks, even after you have gained some proficiency with it yourself. Yet, good timing is at the very core of getting better with horses. I wrote down this chapter's quote in my clinic notebook because it provides a great key to helping understand both when and why to take action in some instances to achieve positive results with a horse.

This chapter's quote was not the first time I had heard Harry share this idea. The concept had been in the forefront of my mind since hearing Harry talk about it at clinics many years before. I also have passed it along to plenty of others during lessons and clinics that I have taught.

By 2015, I felt no urgent need to scribble this quote in my clinic journal since I previously had memorized the concept. I simply reveled in the opportunity to record another instance of Harry sharing it, and I enjoyed capturing his words on the subject again.

So, what is so great about this little quote, anyway? Well, it provides a critical insight. To get a good grasp on it, let's break the quote down so we can work on understanding what Harry means by it.

The first part of the quote states, "If they're getting involved and it affects their emotions...." To put this another way, Harry is saying that if a horse's thought is getting fixed on something other than what the person is presenting, AND it affects the horse's emotions, then...(we will get to what happens after "then" in a minute).

This is a very important idea to consider. Namely that it is one thing for a horse to think about something besides what the person is presenting, but it is something else altogether for the horse to get emotionally wrapped up in it.

On one hoof, I want my horse to be fully aware of what is going on around us and be a real part of a partnership between us. This only happens when my horse has the freedom to think for and express himself. On another hoof, I always want my horse to be mentally available to me regardless of what else may be going on in the environment or his mind. Where a horse's mind sits on the spectrum between these two extremes is extremely important when we go to interact with him.

Sometimes during a clinic I will stand beside a horse and hold a slack lead rope, or sit in the saddle with the reins dropped onto the horse's neck, and talk for a few minutes to the attendees to explain something. At that moment, I'm not asking anything of the horse I'm working with. There remains a connection of feel between us, but it is in neutral and I am not asking the horse to take his thoughts anywhere at that moment.

Sometimes the horse I am with will stand quietly at-ease and get a sleepy look in his eyes. At other times, a horse may turn his head and arch his neck to check something outside the pen somewhere. These kinds of things do not bother me in the least. The horse may have a side-tracked thought, but I am not asking anything of the horse at that moment, so who cares?

I'm not looking to create some militaristic obedience that says the horse can not take a peek away from being at attention, especially when I'm busy talking to other people and not asking anything of him. That seems rather unfair and unnecessary to me—not to mention producing an undesirable feel between us— if he is not acting on his thoughts to the point that he is walking off somewhere or otherwise acting so strongly in relation to those thoughts that he seriously loses track of being with me.

But, if I get ready to ask something of him then I will get a preparedness in my mind and body to do so, and I may engage the lead rope or reins slightly. At that point, I expect the horse to let go of whatever he was checking out—or indeed, wake up and come to the party if he was napping—and be mentally present and completely available to act with me.

If he does not respond by coming back to me as his primary thought right away, then he is emotionally involved in his own wayward thought. As Harry says, I am going to do quite a little in that situation—which means, I'm going to get big enough in some way to break his mind loose from that thought magnet he has become attracted to.

Perhaps a larger than life example may help to illustrate this point. Say I am riding Jubal on a trail and he notices a leopard up ahead in the bushes. I would want him to acknowledge such a threat and cue me into it so that we could collectively save ourselves.

If it turns out that an Appalachian Mountain Leopard (known, of course, to be a ferociously horse-hungry predator) really is up ahead and waiting to pounce on us, then the horse's superior hearing, sight, smell, and instincts may be most useful to saving both of our hind quarters before we stumble into a world of hurt. In such an instance, I would desire Jubal to share this information with me, and maybe even take action. Or at the very least, give me a sure sign that I need to take my thought to what is bothering him.

Now, if it turns out that what Jubal sees really is no more than a perfectly leopard-shaped stump covered by briars (could have fooled anybody...), then this is the exact spot where we find out what is truly going on in our relationship.

Jubal has indicated through his actions and feel that there is a danger up ahead, off to one side of the trail. I have heard him, checked it out, and discerned that it is just a scary looking stump. So I let Jubal know my thoughts on the matter by putting a little firmness on a rein to ask him to leave that thought and tip his head back over onto the line I'm presenting that goes up the trail. With the feel coming from my body we then walk along straight past it.

So, what does Jubal do next?

Well, I'll leave that to your imagination to answer. But whatever your imagination comes up with, it is a legitimate answer and would indicate the current condition of our relationship and the state of training in that horse at that moment.

Which brings us again to part two of Harry's quote, "...I'm going to do quite a little." So, let's explore the meaning of that in greater detail.

Put into context, it means that if a horse gets "emotionally involved" with a thought, then a person needs to "do quite a little" to get the horse to let go of it—that is, get big enough in some way to get the horse to search out something else.

Here is what I mean by saying this is a great concept to

help a person understand the elusive role of good timing in horsemanship. One can know without a doubt that it is necessary to get bigger (perhaps even to have one of those fits we've discussed) when we ask a horse to let go of a thought and he cannot.

With a little work, you can easily feel when a horse who shows things in an obvious way gets involved in a distracted thought. Perhaps his head is high and turned away from where we would like it to be, or he is calling out, or he is prancing around, for example. If you get bigger but do not get big enough to really break through that strong thought, then the horse may feel the need to get even bigger with you. He likely will want to get you out of the way so he can focus on his very important thought. Things could escalate, and you may even witness a horse temper tantrum designed to get you out of his (mental and physical) way.

On the other hand, you can get big enough to break into the horse's reality and become more important than the other thing on his mind and expect to see his focus shift and some relaxation appear in the midst of things. In previous chapters I discussed how getting a horse's mind and body present in the same place at the same time allows the horse to relax. This is another example of that idea. If we can get the horse more in the habit of letting go of strong thoughts in regular life with us (in ideal conditions during training) then we have a chance to have him trust and follow along with us when we suggest that he lets such thoughts go when he thinks we are facing an imaginary Appalachian Mountain Leopard on the trail (in adverse conditions out in the world).

In a horse who is not so grandiose in his expressions, the wayward thought may only be a slight resistance to the rein or lead rope. It is still handled the same way—get big enough to break the horse's mind loose from his thought and work to become his primary focus.

So, when you watch Harry in his riding, or in the groundwork, when a horse gets involved emotionally with something other than what he is presenting, he will "do quite a little." At Mendin' Fences Farm where Harry was working at the time he spoke this chapter's quote, he was working in a round pen that is inside of an arena that is covered by a metal roof. The roof is up on posts that leave the sides open, like a pavilion. The clinic horses are stalled close by but down a steep hill mostly out of sight. Often, horses calling or rattling panels and gates in the stall area is all it takes to get a horse who is being worked quite side-tracked.

Vehicles moving, cows browsing in neighboring fields, or auditors walking around all can cause similar results. These are very useful factors during clinics to help distract a horse who is being worked. Some folks might think such distractions are a nuisance to be avoided. But I have delighted in Harry's approach to these things, which is to use them as opportunities to see where a horse really is in relationship to being able mentally to let go of such things and follow him. And to then work on improving the relationship with the horses who are lacking in this respect.

The timing in how we handle asks and releases with horses is a deep subject, to be sure. But with this quick quote, Harry helps us to see how to test a horse (does he come back mentally when we firm up, for example), and thereby know when to "do quite a little."

For me, this idea again confirms that the horse's mind is what matters most when we address a horse rather than when we simply work on the mechanics of the body as so many horse folks seem to believe. If we get the mind with us, the whole horse is there. If we concentrate mainly on the body, so often the horse's mind is miles away and the results are not great. This can be seen by observing how strongly horses react when their minds are involved emotionally with something. If we break them loose mentally from those things and get them thinking along with us, then we can help a horse become a relaxed, confident, and willing partner.

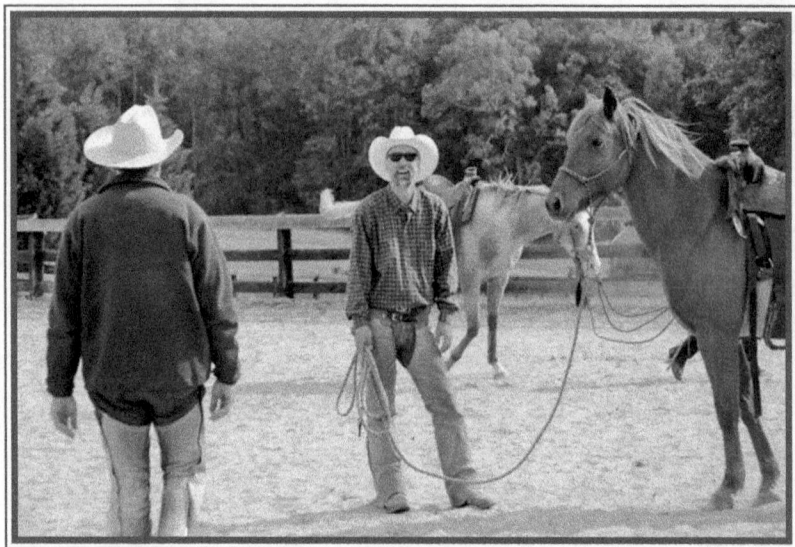

"Pitiful, just Pitiful!" Harry said, as he came into the arena to take the lead rope from me to work with Niji. This photo is a favorite of mine because it really catches the moment of my exasperation as I laugh at the truth of Harry's statement. I had just struggled for some time failing miserably to get Niji's focus with all of the distractions in the arena. When Harry took a hold of the lead rope, he did quite a little bit more to get Niji's mind centered up than I had been doing, and with a great positive change in the gelding. This unfolded on September 24th, 2008 at the very first Virginia Bible/horsemanship clinic; it was held in Hannover County. (Photo: Terry Sparks)

CHAPTER ELEVEN
The Whole Rigmarole

Tuesday, 27 August, 2019—Bible/Horsemanship Clinic, Floyd, Virginia.

"If all you're doing is making it happen, it is not a benefit to you; it's not changing the [horse's] mind," Harry declared.

Harry's statement prefacing this chapter embodies a fundamental idea that is important to consider when undertaking anything with a horse. One can focus on making the horse's body do things or one can focus on the horse's mind and ask the horse to think along with a request from the person and thus position his own equine body accordingly—and the two are very different.

The difference between making a horse do something and having a horse engage willingly with a suggestion from a person is profound. It is profound in both how the horse thinks and feels about the interaction with the human and in how the horse reacts to a request. Often I think of this in terms of mechanical versus willing actions in horses. Hallmarks of the former are stiff, high-headed, worried movements, and the latter produces more soft, relaxed qualities in the horse's body. One is a forced, physical focus and manipulation, and the other is a more mental undertaking that constitutes communication.

It is not an overstatement to say that really getting through to the horse's mind is the underlying foundation of any excellent horse/human interactions, either by design or by accident. Of course, we desire for it to be intentional—that we might own it, understand it, and use it with consistency and enjoy horses who show the better results for it. If we can gain such progress through study and application, we call it horsemanship. (Well, other approaches get called "horsemanship," too, but I prefer this version of it!)

When Harry made the statement above at a clinic, he was referring specifically to the "rigmarole." The rigmarole provides a great example to explore this idea, even if it is a little complicated.

The rigmarole is a term that got applied to a certain choreography of moves that Harry sometimes uses with horses. The story of how this bit of horse maneuvering got its moniker is that there was a gal riding with Harry in a clinic years ago. He was coaching her on how to line up these moves and get her horse's mind to come through in the process. After a number of failed attempts, she asked, "Do I have to do the whole rigmarole again?" And it stuck.

The most straightforward way to share the rigmarole is to discuss it in the realm of a rider on a horse, although variations can be done in ground work or when working one horse from another. The rider begins a rigmarole by picking up a rein. In general, every time a rein is engaged it is important to have the horse's mind likewise become engaged in the direction of the rein and that we not release that rein until the horse is thinking along with it. Without this consistency in handling the reins—if we release a rein, say, for a step but without the horse really thinking about stepping in said direction (a "mechanical" application of the reins)—then we undo the benefit of establishing the reins for willingness and thoughtful operation. The rigmarole is intended (among other things, like getting a horse to rebalance through his body) to get the horse really thinking along with the reins.

Let's take a perfect scenario first to show what a rigmarole looks like in its refined state. The rider starts by picking up a rein. The rider guides the horse to think around in the direction of that rein. The horse hears the rein, takes a good strong look around in the direction following the feel on the rein and the rider brings the rein around in front of herself and brings her hand holding the rein across the center line (across the saddle horn on a western saddle). The horse continues to follow the feel presented on the rein around beautifully bending through his neck and body. At some point, he looks around so far that his own posterior is in the way of his thought tracking the rein. When this happens, the horse moves his butt out of the way so he can continue to think around with the human's offer on the rein; thereby, stepping his hind quarters over. If the right rein is the one engaged, the horse's hind end will step to the left.

At the moment the horse commits to stepping his hind end over, the rider gives a partial release to say, "Yes, that's what I'm looking for; thank you." Then there is a moment where the horse is in a semi-neutral state, but still attentive, and the rein remains partially engaged. The rider now moves the hand with the engaged rein out to its side (so in our example, the right rein is moved out to the right of the horse) and offers a feel for the horse to think out in that direction. The horse, being perfect in this example, follows this feel willingly, and the rider offers strong enough on the rein to the right that the horse—perfectly balanced—steps his front end laterally to the right pivoting on the hind.

Having just completed a beautiful rigmarole, the rider releases the rein and rides off into the sunset with a light arc to the right at first, and then straightening out to an energetic walk, the horse's head low, legs reaching, head and rib cage swinging freely...perfect!

That's the rigmarole.

And now for a picture of what it usually looks like when a rider begins to work on the rigmarole with a horse who is unfamiliar with it. And let's look at how working on the rigmarole can help make the difference between training a horse that is willing versus one who is mechanical.

Our not-so-refined rigmarole begins the same way as the ideal example—the rider picks up a rein. We'll stick with the right rein since it went so well above. But this horse's head flies up when he feels pressure on the rein and he resists by bracing against the bit (or side-pull). Our esteemed rider, however, is a seasoned veteran of the rigmarole and she knows how to deal with this situation. She holds onto the rein, not yanking the horse's head around, but not releasing either. She merely holds the pressure in a way that it is the horse who is pulling against her and not the other way around.

The horse struggles at this for a while, but finding that the rider isn't like others he has known and isn't letting go of the rein, he figures he'll try taking a step forward. Surely that's what the rider wants, right? A step?

Well, yes and no. Ultimately the goal is to get the horse to step his front end to the right if the person asks through the right rein for that. But, our accomplished rider isn't interested in any steps that do not have the horse's mind truly thinking along in the proper direction. So she holds out and does not release for the forward step.

The horse becomes rather frustrated at this human who doesn't understand how this deal works and should have let go of the rein by now. The step does show he is trying other things besides just pulling back against the rein. This search is a good thing. In fact, if a horse doesn't begin to search and try different things our expert rider knows she must increase her firmness on the rein by degrees to see about getting the horse to search. The horse next tries taking a step backwards to see if that will get rid of the annoying right rein. Nope, that doesn't work either. Finally, the horse tries looking in the direction of the rein.

Several things happen when the horse looks in the direction of the right rein. First, since our acclaimed rider is not pulling on the rein to force the horse to turn his head but rather it is the

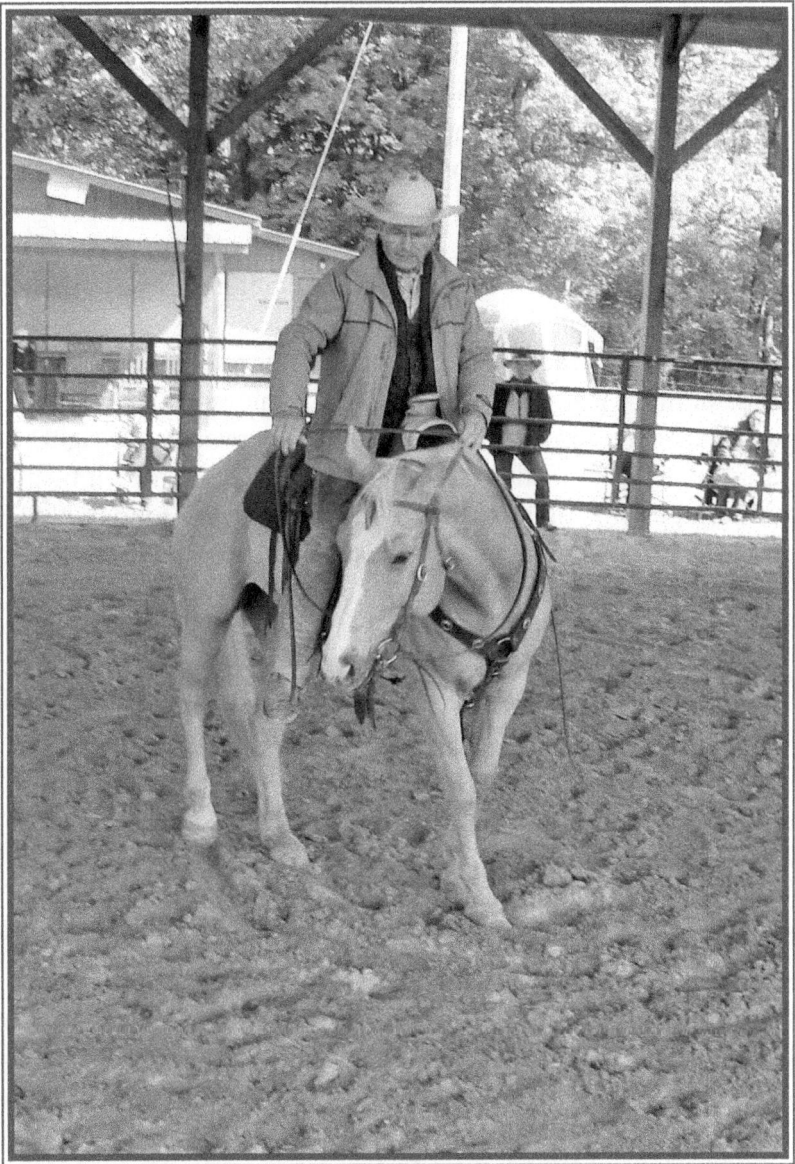

In this photo from May 18, 2014 at Mendin' Fences Farm in Rogersville, Tennessee Harry and Moxy are in the final stages of a rigmarole as he offers the gelding (owned by Connie Crawford) to step his front end over to the right.

horse who is pulling back against the feel offered by the rider on the rein, the horse instantly put slack in the rein himself. He thereby provided himself the release he desired—which, by the way, the rider was offering all along if he would just think to the right. The horse also softened and lowered his head with the release of the rein because he now is looking in the direction of the right rein because his mind has let go of all the other thoughts he was having and he has tried thinking along in the direction of the rein offered by the person.

Now, our revered rider understands how much of a struggle her poor horse just went through and she knows that this is a good learning moment. She goes ahead and releases the right rein completely and offers a sweet spot of feel from herself to her horse, petting him on the neck and giving him a moment to process what just took place. In this way she has abandoned the rigmarole temporarily to help establish a good spot between her horse and her and thus help provide some critically needed extra good feeling after the release.

With that accomplished, it's time to go further and see about getting to the whole rigmarole with this horse. Starting with the right rein again, our highly-regarded rider gets the horse to turn his head on the end of his neck to the right, take a good strong look around in that direction, and bend through his neck and body to the right. This is looking great! But when she offers a touch more to see if the horse can step the right foot out laterally to the right, the horse steps, but he steps forward again. This isn't the horse really thinking to the right, and shows that the horse is thinking more forward and is likely on the forehand with his weight. This is a somewhat "autopilot" response where the horse just throws something out there to try and placate the rider to get rid of the pressure on the rein.

To address this forward step, the rider brings her right hand that holds the right rein across in front of her and slightly upwards in the direction of her left shoulder. The horse resists against it, but he also searches for a way to get a release from the pressure on the rein. Eventually, the horse thinks around enough with the right rein that he steps his hind quarters out of the way. That is was what the rider was looking for, so she offers a partial release on the right rein. At this point, the rider switches from asking the horse to step the hindquarters over to reaching out and asking for the horse to step the front end laterally to the right.

Perhaps the horse will make it. If the horse does step laterally to the right with his front end, the rider will release and ride off. But, especially early on when attempting the rigmarole with a horse who is unfamiliar with it, the horse is just as likely to try stepping forward again and again. Horses are such forward thinkers that it can be tough to get them to let go of their habitual thought of going forward at the first chance they have. If the horse steps forward, the rider will again bring the rein all the way around and across the centerline in front of her and disengage the horse's hind end.

When the rider gets the hind end to step over, she again offers the rein out to the side to see about getting the horse to really think out that way and step the front end laterally. The horse either comes through with the front lateral step or not, which in turn means the rider either releases and rides on or goes again to disengage the hind quarters.

It's not hard to see how this dance got its name and a student of Harry's might, after however-so-many of these maneuvers, rather desperately ask, "Do I have to do the whole rigmarole again?" But the answer is yes if we want the benefits it can bring about for the horse. With consistency, time, and the rewards of a more relaxed and better-feeling horse, a person can use the rigmarole to help support a horse into the habit of thinking along with the reins and thus with the rider.

This also can help produce a horse who rebalances himself to be able to quickly and with less or no tension perform a wider range of tasks with a rider. The horse begins to understand that a range of requests might be made of him at any time and that he is capable and better off to be balanced and prepared mentally and physically to simply follow the rider's feel and partner with the rider in whatever is asked of him. This situation helps along the way to what Harry calls "with-you-ness."

There is quite a depth of intricacies that can be discussed that go on within the rigmarole, but to keep this chapter to a reasonable length I want to keep the focus on Harry's opening remarks. He spoke that statement because one aspect of the rigmarole is that a rider can force the rigmarole movements to happen rather than allowing the horse to come through in them with his own thinking—and as Harry points out, when the rider forces the movements rather than waiting on the horse to come through, "it is not a benefit to you."

A mechanical rigmarole almost certainly is a much faster way to get the moves accomplished. A person can rock the horse backwards by pulling on the reins to get the horse's weight off the front end, pull the horse's head around with a rein, dig a heel into the horse's flank to get the hind end to disengage, and then with the opposite leg in tandem with the reins, drive the horse's front end over laterally, and there you have it—all of the movements we are looking for in a jiffy! But the horse had no say-so in that. A horse can be looking hard in the very opposite direction the rider wants him to move in and still the horse can reluctantly move his body to get away from physical driving forces inflicted by the rider. But that approach has no true benefit because the horse hasn't changed his mind to a new understanding that brings about relaxation, willingness, with-you-ness, and other positives.

When things are set up as in our two examples, the rider puts the horse in just enough of a bind that the horse begins to search and to think for himself how to cope with the situation. The horse tries this and that, and when he comes to think along with the rein, rebalance himself, step the hind or front end per the rider's request...well, that represents a mental involvement of going with what is presented that will not be present if the rider simply physically manipulates the horse's body (where the horse is primarily getting away from a rider's pressure).

In fact, physically driving the horse's body parts can have an ill effect on the horse. It can create something along the lines of resentment or reluctance. It can cause a horse to desire to be elsewhere other than with the rider so strongly that it is common to see horses doing anything they can within their captive condition to get away. Such horse behaviors as looking away from the direction the rider wishes to go in, shutting down with eyes glazing over to mentally go elsewhere, lifting the head high, bracing the mouth, head, neck, and body, and bucking the rider off are not uncommon reactions to mechanically manipulating horses.

On the other hoof, rigmaroles conducted with patience are time well spent because the rider has a chance to provide consistent handling that can allow the horse to come to important conclusions on his own. At first, the horse typically attempts a variety of things in response to the rider's requests. If the horse has a history with humans, and some poor, mechanical handling in particular, it even can be quite frustrating before any new understanding is established. But when the horse's various efforts do or don't work out to gain a release, it is the horse who feels like he came to them on his own. The process seems to be both empowering and calming to horses.

It is easy for me to become rather passionate about the subject of the rigmarole. That is because I've seen a great many horses forced into their motions, and I have seen many wonderful examples of how that kind of relationship with humans can be changed to one of willingness and reduced tensions for the horse. It is certainly a much better deal for the human, too. Reflecting on the opening quote from Harry, it is obvious where Harry's mind is on this subject. In his opinion, simply making horses move certain ways is not a real benefit because his interest is completely tied to helping horses feel better and more relaxed in their interactions with humans. I have also heard Harry say on many occasions, "A horse doesn't perform his best unless he's feeling his best."

The rigmarole is an amazing horsemanship tool, and there is much more that could be expounded about it than this chapter provides. But for now, I hope a basic overview of the rigmarole demonstrates how different it is to make a horse do something versus setting things up so the horse feels like he came to some conclusions on his own.

CHAPTER TWELVE
Guiding a Search

Thursday, 27 May, 2010—Mendin' Fences Farm, Rogersville, Tennessee.

"If you don't give them an opportunity, you won't know if they are going to make it or not," Harry said.

Many horses get micromanaged by their people. As a species we humans can be an overbearing bunch with our desires for obedience in our pets, other people, and certainly horses, as well. The thing about obedience is that, while it may produce behaviors one desires in another creature, these behaviors can be contrived, or even forced, and that has relationship consequences. Obedience is not the same as a willingness to follow another. It is important to understand the difference between the two as they relate to horsemanship.

It is quite common to see horses under saddle going through the motions with a rider or being forced to perform in a mechanical/physical way. Such horses show signs that speak volumes of how they would rather be somewhere else. Nervousness and tension, dullness and glazed-over eyes, bolting and bucking...all these clues and others point to a horse who would rather be elsewhere than with the human at that moment.

Harry's words for this chapter conjure up a bunch of examples in my mind of horses who are accustomed to owners making them do things without having the opportunity for input themselves. The situation that prompted Harry to speak this chapter's quote is a great example as well.

A person was working a horse loose in the round pen. Harry was coaching her to help get the horse drawing to her, and she was using a flag. There had been some progress. The horse at first had been trotting around the pen out by the panels. With some well-timed flagging, the person had the horse doing okay at turning in and walking towards her, and now the horse was drawing in close enough to her and standing so that she could pet the horse on the face. At this point, Harry was having the

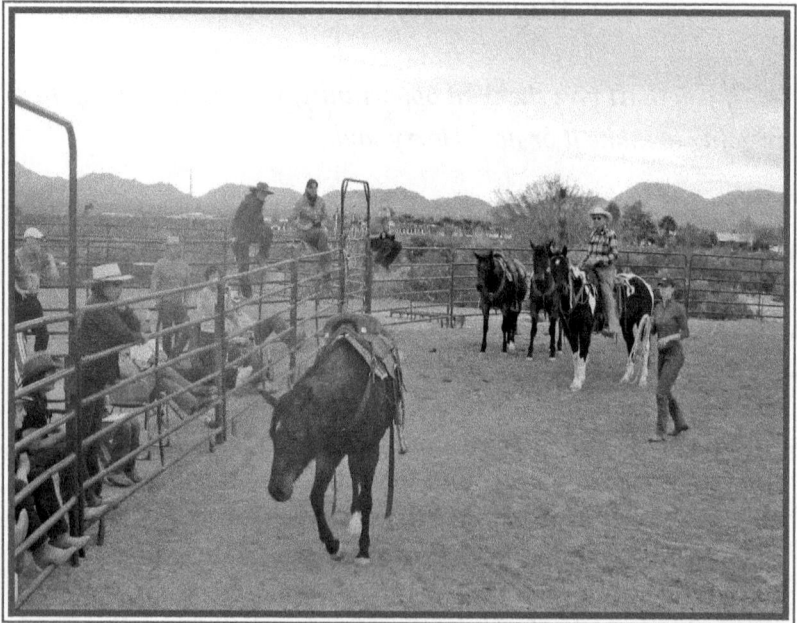

Harry atop Easy on February 18, 2014, with Sky, Tinker, and Bailey newly saddled during the one and only Harry Whitney Colt Starting clinic. Anna Bonnage is afoot in the arena helping Harry, and the crowd of auditors looks on. The 92 pages of notes I took at this clinic added significantly to my clinic journal collection and was part of the basis for my Six Colts, Two Weeks trilogy that ultimately took eight years to complete.

person send the horse away from her a step or two to see if the horse could stay connected and draw back to her right away.

With the person in the middle of the round pen and the horse standing and facing her, she would tip the horse's thought out to one side and then bring up her energy so that the horse would step off in that direction. She then would stop and try to draw the horse back to her.

The horse had a tendency to step around 180 degrees from the owner and head towards the fence panels. Harry coached the person to be prepared to flag if the horse became committed to leaving her mentally altogether. The timing of any flagging was intended to remind the horse that the person remained close by. It likewise was both a call for the horse to let go of the thought away from the person and also an ask that the horse draw back in to her again.

But as soon as the horse turned 180 degrees and took a step away from the owner, the owner would flag the horse. The horse would react by increasing his speed away from the person, going out to the panels, and then running along the panels.

Harry pointed out that the owner was not giving the horse a real chance to make a decision to draw back to her before she flagged. In this instance, the premature flagging drove the horse away from the person even stronger (the opposite of what was sought) rather than allowing the horse time enough to make the decision about whether to turn back to the person or to really commit to going away.

Harry suggested that if the horse got all the way to the panels without turning back, that it was a pretty safe bet that he was mentally gone, and the owner should flag. When the person improved at allowing the horse time to make a decision before intervening, pretty soon she was rewarded with the horse willingly turning back to her every time.

Observing this session, I took home that when a person flags too soon there is little chance for a horse to turn in because the early flagging simply does not allow it—so be careful in general not to block the very thing that is sought by trying to make it happen right now. Give the horse room to "make a mistake" (try whatever is on his mind) and then intervene and make that not work out so well if the horse is truly committed to it rather than try to force the horse to conform to what is wanted.

This idea applies to many things that we might do with a horse. When picking up a rein, for example, a person can offer a feel and hold it for the horse's thought to come through to that side or one can use the rein mechanically and pull the horse's head around. Offering a feel on a lead rope for a horse to go and circle a person is likewise very different in feel and result than taking the end of a lead rope and spinning it in a threatening way at a horse's hind end to make him go forward. The list goes on and on.

The point is that "*if you don't give them an opportunity, you won't know if they are going to make it or not*." Giving a horse the opportunity to do something means just that—being willing to set things up and waiting for the horse to come through. This may require time and patience. But more than that, this requires an understanding of what the two different approaches look and feel like. One of the frustrating things about horsemanship is that so many things can depend on so many things: the horse, the environment, what a person is asking...it's always a moving target.

So what does giving a horse an opportunity to make a choice in decision-making matters look and feel like? Well, I think for some people it feels like jumping over the edge of a cliff into a great abyss. Relinquishing control, especially control of a large animal that is to be climbed atop and ridden, is no small concern. It takes courage, work, and a new understanding to break old habits, give a horse a chance to explore his options, and breathe new life into the dynamic between the horse and the human by guiding a search rather than by trying to make something be.

Harry often speaks about "setting up a search" in a horse. It has been extremely helpful for me to think of this idea when I ask something of a horse. It boils down to the fact that we really cannot make a horse have a thought. Rather, what we do is have something in mind for our horse to do and then we "block" (discourage) other thoughts that the horse has until he happens to try the one we are looking for. Then we make that one work out really well. Although we have guided the search, in essence the horse did come up with the idea we wanted him to have on his own through the searching process, and he knows this. Carry this process along to the relationship at large and not only do we get our horse to understand specific things—like when we pick up the right rein the horse thinks to the right—but, the horse can develop an understanding of (and gain confidence in) the process itself.

When the horse understands this process in general, new asks from the person are not so troubling to a horse. They are not because the horse becomes confident that there is something he can do to restore his balance again with the person and it will make the ask go away. A horse who has been handled in this way with consistency should begin to search for what is needed to get a release from a person's ask rather than become more tense, panic, or in some way shut down or hit flight mode.

Horses like to be in balance with other horses, with people, and with their surroundings. When a person puts some feel on a rein, that is an imbalance in the horse's world, and the horse wants it gone and to be back to neutral again. The horse will do what he can to get rid of that imbalance. This is why reins work. The rein changes the position of a bit or side-pull so that it no longer rests in a balanced way on the horse and this can cause the horse to reposition his entire body to get lined up with the bit and between the reins again.

A very important point to keep in mind is that what a person releases for is what the horse learns works out to get his balance back with a person in a given situation. If the horse feels a rein being engaged and he rears up and the person lets go, well... the horse just figured out how to regain his neutral state with regards to the rein. Or if the horse figures out that if he swings his bum around so that his head faces the direction of the rein being engaged and the person releases, that is what he will take home as what to do when a rein is used. Or if a person does not release and allow the horse to go back to neutral until the horse really looks, thinks, and steps the front end in the direction of the engaged rein, then that is what will become established in the horse's mind.

When you think about this, a few points become evident. One is that there is no problem with a horse searching and trying different things to discover what will return the neutral state when a person presents an ask to the horse. There should not be punishment for the horse trying what comes natural for him to do first when we ask something of him, even if it is way off our hopeful list. If a horse is not searching, a person needs to do enough to get a search happening—up the intensity of the ask enough to get the horse's mind engaged and at least working on it.

And we should not box a horse in and manage him so tightly that it is impossible for him to try things. Searching allows us to see what is high on the horse's list of things to try and allows the horse to mark the "wrong" ones off the list himself. If we don't allow the horse the opportunity to try a variety of things, he may hold out hope to eventually try them which can get in the way of a willingness we seek to have with the horse.

A great example of this is the barn-sour horse—a horse who, when ridden away from the barn, only wants to return to the barn as soon, and perhaps as quickly (!), as possible. This situation can be perpetual and present unpleasantries with every ride for years as a horse hopes to get back to the barn ASAP. What works to help improve or resolve this trouble is not fighting on-and-on forever with a horse to leave the barn and go somewhere, but rather to just drop the reins and let him go back to the barn—just let him go try it once and for all. At first, that may seem like giving in to the horse's "wrong" choice and teaching the opposite of what one hopes to achieve. The key, though, is to let the horse go all the way back to the barn and then ask the horse do a bit of work there.

Trot some circles or figure eights at the barn. You don't have to make it the worst experience ever (remember, you will want him to go back to the barn at some point), just make a little work for him there. Then direct him away from the barn and walk out gently a little ways and drop the reins. If he turns and takes you right back to the barn, just let him do it and repeat the trotting or whatever work you have going there at the barn and then ride out easy away from the barn again and drop the reins.

Eventually, most horses decide for themselves that the barn really isn't all that it's cracked up to be and they let go of the strong urge to get back there. When this happens, "out there" becomes the spot where the horse finds the tranquil balance he desires and a rider can direct the horse to go explore new places with newfound freedom and willingness.

The relationship that builds through the application of horsemanship certainly can go in a variety of directions depending on what our style of "horsemanship" is. Allowing horses the freedom to explore options and helping them to then cross the undesirable ones off the list is a good way to engage with their minds. This fits the theme of this book, which is that to truly improve our relationships to horses we must focus on their mental focus rather than simply making their physical bodies do things. It is, perhaps, a bit ironic that by letting horses go and explore the things we aren't asking for we actually provide the situation that can have a horse eventually following us in a willing and interested way.

When I think of this chapter's quote from Harry, I always think of myself in the horse's hooves. How does it feel to me when I am condemned as guilty for something—even a small thing—before I have the chance to really sort out what I am going to do? I have experienced this and it feels lousy and causes resentment. I don't know if horses feel resentment like humans do, but I do know that they can hang onto ill feelings of some kind that also cause undesirable actions if they are made to act without having a chance to try some options of their own. And we do them a disservice, and are forcing our will on them, when we neglect to give them the chance to come up with "right" choices or not.

So it leaves me with the Golden Rule in mind—that I do unto horses as I would like to have done unto me. I'd like to be given a chance to sort things out for myself, have the chance to take in some ideas from others when available, and not be forced to do something without consideration of my own input. Horses are like this, too. So to achieve the kind of relationship I am looking for with horses, I need to keep this in mind and allow horses the same consideration.

CHAPTER THIRTEEN

Setting Up a Search or Blocking a Thought

Thursday, 25 May, 2011—Mendin' Fences Farm, Rogersville, Tennessee.

"It's almost always better if we can let horses go try something and we convince them it doesn't work out so well than to block it completely; but there are times where blocking is prudent," Harry said.

The above quote is a fine follow-up to the previous chapter. The first part of what Harry says here again stresses the importance of allowing a horse to search for what we are asking. But this time, Harry added another bit of advice, *"but there are times where blocking is prudent."*

I've heard Harry speak many times about the difference between boundaries and requests as relates to working with horses. Understanding this differentiation has been extremely beneficial to me. It is a way to think about when it is okay to firm up and really block a horse's thought and when the greatest benefit is found in allowing a horse time to search for what we are asking.

One of the easiest ways to begin to understand this for me was to think about working with a colt who has had minimal experience with a human. If a horse has not been handled much, he has little to no frame of reference for what a person asks of him or of the process of getting that relationship established. Therefore, it is really important to provide plenty of time for the young horse to begin to understand what an ask feels like and to learn how to find out what it means and how to get a release from it.

For instance, one of the first things I may do with a colt when handling him is to slip the end of a rope over the young horse's neck with plenty of slack. I bring that loose end back to my hand making a large loop around the horse's neck that I can release instantly to avoid a wreck by just opening my hand if the colt pulls strongly away.

Once this loop is in place, I will apply just an ounce of pressure on the side of the horse's neck opposite me by moving the loop towards me. This is a way of asking the colt to look towards me. This can take some time at first, though not always. When the colt does give a look my way, I release the feel on the rope by moving the hand holding the loop slightly towards the horse which puts the loop slack around his neck.

Pretty soon, if all goes well, I can put a little more feel on that rope around the neck and get the youngster to take a step towards me. I am not pulling the horse towards me, but rather I am offering a feel and waiting for the horse to think about and decide to step towards me—there's a big difference between those two options.

Often I have the youngster standing beside his mother for support, and the step the colt takes is one away from her side and towards me. It is not a process to be hurried, and with time and patience the positive experience and consistency of that work can build into a nice bit of feel and communication that can be built upon. One hopes to get two steps, then three, then eventually be leading the colt away from mom and then back to her in a quick circle, and so on.

In this photo, I am in Pulaski, Virginia working with a young colt named Jubal (not my Jubal, but a client's horse also named Jubal) on June 12, 2016. The colt is standing beside his mother. The youngster is feeling okay about the lariat over his neck. I made a loop by holding the end of the lariat back onto the rope so that I can let go and he'll be free if the need arises. With plenty of slack in the loop, I put a touch of feel on it so the outside of that loop presses up against his neck on his right side and I work to draw his thought to me. This went very well and soon I was able to draw his mind to me, then a step, and pretty soon I was able to have him walking away from the mare, around me, and then back to mom without any issues. Soon, I was able to lead him further away from the mare and right back to her without a problem. It is always thrilling to have these early moments go well!

But, for example, if the colt wants to push on me (this can be as small as a mental push from a distance or as big as physically attempting to push on me) I am going to block that absolutely in a means big enough and right away so that it does not work out. That is a boundary—it's not going to happen and there is going to be complete clarity in that. I don't want a colt pushing on me, and I surely don't want that behavior getting established to where a grown horse has a habit of pushing on people, so that needs to be built into the relationship with no ambiguity.

It may be confusing to the onlooker to see because at a time where I am working hard to be relatively quiet and draw a colt's thought to me, I may block a pushy thought towards me hard enough that the colt goes away from me strongly. But as a boundary, pushing on me is not something I am going to allow from the very beginning. The horse can sort out the difference. The horse knows when he pushes on me, and he knows whether I yielded to it or did not allow it and all that such an interaction means in terms of how our relationship will be established. So, it should not become a set back.

I think setting a boundary does not create a set back, at least in part, because it falls in line with how horses interact with one another in the herd. Horses can set boundaries with one another without residual problems being created. Sometimes these boundaries can be established with pretty big expressions, like kicking or biting, but usually once done it's over and there seems to be no lingering trouble in it. Horses seem to be matter-of-fact about it and, unlike humans, they do not get very emotional about the process. So often when people go to set a boundary, they can get angry about it—mad at the horse and taking something the horse did in a personal way when for the horse it is just a horse being a horse and not at all personal.

I bring this up to say that whatever we do to with a horse, whether it be setting a boundary or making a request, it goes much better if we keep our emotions out of it. If a horse is struggling already with a situation, a person getting emotional, especially angry, will only cause the horse to be more worried, confused, and dubious of the human. That won't help matters at a time when a horse is better served by support and being guided with clear and consistent signals from a person.

A request, as opposed to a boundary, involves a search that can build to greater understanding over time and improve with many repetitions.

"Prudent" is the operative word in deciding what should be a request and what should be a boundary. Safety for both the human and the horse is certainly one important criterion for setting boundaries. A pushy horse, to use our example above, is not safe. Therefore, it is prudent and makes sense that we should block pushy-ness as a boundary. But in general, what we ask of our horses are requests.

I like for a horse to be able to back up off the feel on a lead rope, for instance. The process to get that working is to begin by putting the feel on the lead rope for the horse to back up as I would like it to be in the perfect world. For me, that is an almost imperceptible up and down wiggle. Of course, the unfamiliar horse will not understand what this means, but the horse will recognize it even if he does not react to it. Then, I get bigger with the wiggle and feel on the rope until pretty quickly I get a backwards step, and I then release.

In this process, the horse has had a chance to notice and react to the very light offer to back, but at first this light request is easily ignored. The escalation that I present next is big enough to get the horse trying something. At first, the horse may try a sideways step—and if he has been quite stuck I may release for that as at least some kind of breakthrough. Pretty soon, though, I will not release for that and will expect a backwards step for a release. If I am consistent with offering the light ask ahead of the bigger requests, the horse should begin to hear that slight wiggle and be backing because he understand what it means and he knows he might as well back because the escalation will follow if he doesn't. He becomes more attentive to my requests, which only can happen if he is thinking about them—thus I have his mind focused with my requests and me.

There are many great examples of seeing requests build towards an easy understanding between horse and human. Getting a horse to load into a trailer is a great one. There can be quite a bit of time involved in getting a horse to load in a trailer...maybe even work over a number of days. The situation can be set up so that the horse is brought to the trailer and the offer is given that he think inside the box. If he doesn't, some pressure can be added by making smooching noises or flagging or slapping a chap with a rope or some such ask. Then when he does think inside, the person gets very quiet and offers a sweet spot to make it work out very well. Then over time, the ask can be applied and maintained until there is a foot on the ramp before getting a release, then a foot in the trailer door, then two, then four—and when the horse backs out before he is all the way in the trailer, let him go try that and see for himself how it works out. But that causes the ask to come in there again with another release only when he again thinks forward inside the trailer. Eventually, you have a horse who understands the situation and hopefully loads willingly.

Similarly, a request can be set up for a horse to sidle up by a gate to be mounted, or to step onto a stump, or to leg yield, or to bow...to do so many things. But in the process of establishing every one of these, the horse no doubt will have other ideas he would rather do than what we have in mind along the way. Harry is saying that in a request go ahead and let the horse try whatever he comes up with to discover for himself that it is not going to work out. But just keep in mind that there may be times it is sensible to block a thought hard and fast.

To share another of Harry's sayings that sheds some light on this, "It is not the thoughts that a horse is willing to let go of that get us in trouble; it is the ones that they can't let go of that get us in trouble."

Thus perhaps the greatest benefit we can provide our horses is to help them learn to let go of a thought. In the course of our work with horses, blocking pushiness, blocking a thought that is about to turn into a buck and get a rider in peril, blocking a pinned-eared snarky thought to bite a person...there are times it is prudent to block those hard and fast without allowing the search. However, as people can be awfully quick to look for obedience and conformity rather than willingness and with-you-ness from horses, it is important not to take this idea and run too far with it. Yes, there are times it is prudent to block a horse's thought, but don't let everything become "prudent." The time put into setting up searches is where the willingness really gets going with a horse.

I was at a clinic of Harry's in Montana one summer and I watched him use a stock whip to help Sunshine, a horse owned by Linda Davenport, search out in a round pen to come to him and be relaxed and willing about it. That session ended up becoming the subject of a whole chapter in the book *Going Somewhere* as I was intrigued by how something as scary as a stock whip cracking like gun shots could be used to help a horse search and find to become increasingly relaxed and more with the person cracking the whip. But with good timing and no emotionally loaded cracks at the horse (only matter-of-fact cracks in the center of the pen never intended to drive the horse anywhere), that horse searched, tried this and that, and was guided by well timed releases to come right up to the whip-cracker and get petted and be close to him where Sunshine clearly felt better than anywhere else in the pen. It took maybe an hour or more, so not a ton of time in the big picture, but what a change for the better in that horse. It seemed like after that experience, anything could have happened in the environment and Sunshine would have been heading for Harry for support and done so willingly.

So again, with horses it all depends! Setting up a search and blocking are two very different approaches, but there are times to use each of these. We can apply ourselves to the task of learning when one is right for a given horse in a given situation and when it may be better to employ the other. Understanding the difference between the two and considering the two options is certainly a big step towards becoming more handy in horsemanship.

CHAPTER FOURTEEN

Horse Troubles

Tuesday, 27 August, 2019— Bible/Horsemanship Clinic, Floyd, Virginia.

"It's the thoughts a horse won't let go of that get us in trouble," Harry remarked.

It is, of course, horse troubles that cause us horse folks grief. Horse troubles motivate us to go to clinics, devour books and videos on horsemanship, take riding lessons, and to do whatever we can to get handy enough to remedy those difficulties. Also, we want our horses to feel the best they can and be worry free, safe, and fun to ride and interact with. This chapter's quote holds the key to all of that.

I just made a reference to this quote of Harry's in the last chapter, so now seems like a great time to address it. When I met Harry, I began to see how horses' thoughts being focused with humans or not causes things to go well or poorly between horses and people. It was then that I began to get the traction that I longed for to advance my horsemanship in a truly meaningful way. In fact, even after making progress and knowing full well the truth of Harry's above statement, when I have had horse troubles, it always circles back around to the fact that I am not getting the horse's mind with me.

The first book I wrote after I met Harry and began learning from him was *A Horse's Thought*. The title of that book is telling. It makes it pretty obvious that from the very beginning of my learning experiences with Harry that I clearly grasped his main message to his students, that having a horse's thought with you is at the very core of effective horsemanship and developing a real relationship with horses.

So back to the quote. It is a simple statement, and really not hard to comprehend on the surface. Yet, as simple as the premise is, it seems that we humans struggle very hard to latch onto it and use it as a fundamental basis for truly bettering our relationships with horses. Let's explore.

(I should note here that I am not talking about trouble in horses caused by physical issues, like pain or illness—that would be in a different category—but rather I am addressing behavioral/relationship based issues.)

What does trouble with a horse look like? Well, it is easy to conjure up all kinds of images, isn't it? But what they all have in common—from the horse that is reluctant to be led, to the horse that is bucking a person off, to every other large or small horse trouble—is that the horse has an idea in his head that he thinks is so important that he must focus on it, entirely or in part, overtop of anything else that the human might be presenting. To be causing trouble in the horse/human relationship, the horse's thought must be strong enough that he can not easily let it go and get on board with something else that the human is presenting to him to do.

In contrast, horses' thoughts that are easily and willingly let go of do not become issues for people. This is because a horse simply lets them go when a person asks something else of a horse. There is no conflict of horse interest when the mind of the horse is free to follow what a person offers.

Therefore, our best efforts should be applied to engage our horses in ways that convince them to let go of their thoughts and be guided to try the ones that we offer they go with. When they do, horses can become peaceful and willing, and be directed by a person because the horses' minds are not in turmoil. And when a horse's mind is not bothered, his actions likewise become more peaceful, soft, and steady.

That sounds straightforward and rational enough. And yet it is completely common to see a human acting without taking a horse's thoughts into account. Over and over again I witness people making horses do things without the slightest notion of where the horse's thoughts are—which usually are strongly elsewhere. And, I will be the first to admit that I was doing that very thing before I met Harry and began to see the tremendous benefits to how he approached horses. It is typical to see horses' minds off-tasks, from the backyard trail horse to the multi-million dollar winners of every equestrian sport. It is not an exaggeration to say that it simply is not characteristic of human nature to consider horses' minds when working with them.

I want to add a note here addressing some applications of what is largely called natural horsemanship. The mechanical pressure and release training that is popular with many clinicians and students of natural horsemanship does not necessarily engage the horse's mind in a way that I am describing in this chapter. Driving a horse into actions and then giving a release from that physical pressure, as they often do, is not the same thing as offering a feel for a horse to go with and then offering a sweet spot and release from an ask when the horse arrives at the right idea himself.

I often use the example of a horse being worked in a round pen for the first time to show the difference between the two approaches. It is common to see a natural horsemanship advocate drive a horse around the pen, sometimes very hard, and then back off the pressure to suck the horse in towards the person. That is very different from simply standing in the middle of the round pen with a worried horse running around by the panels and the person doing something occasionally to say, "Hey horse, I'm over here in the middle, and when you're

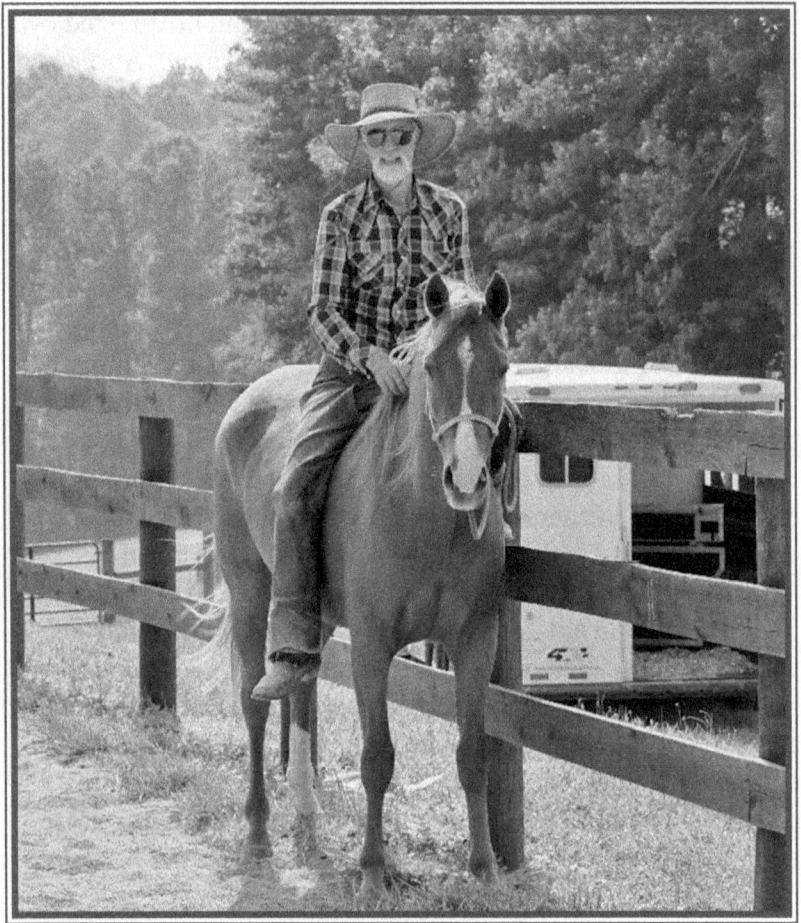

Newly, my recently acquired two-year-old gelding, got to come to the second week of the 2023 Bible/horsemanship clinic that we host each year here in Virginia. This photo is from August 22 and shows the first time I sat astride Newly. We had been working on some ground work in the busy arena that afternoon and, although it wasn't planned, the opportunity presented itself and everything felt right, so I slipped off the fence onto his back and what-da-ya-know, a wonderful non-event. Harry saw us and snapped this photo to commemorate the exciting woohoo moment, and it got quite a bit of coverage in my current clinic journal, let me tell you! (Photo: Harry Whitney)

ready to let go of the thought of running around with your mind outside of the pen you can find peace and rest when you focus with me over here."

That isn't to say that some considerable, and even quite quick, achievements *from a human perspective* can't be made through a mechanical means of approaching horsemanship. But if we look at things from the horse's point of view, mostly what is produced when horses are worked without consideration for where their minds are focused are horses who are resistant and thinking hard about getting somewhere else rather than being with the human on a task at hand.

Think about riding a horse, for example. You are on a horse and heading out on a trail ride alone into a wooded area. Before you even reach the trail, just leaving the barn you can feel the horse getting anxious. Right from the start there is a concerning feeling and tension that most anybody who has any horse experience has felt and wished would go away. Why is that feeling coming up in that horse? Because the horse isn't mentally present with the rider and willing to be directed. There is a distinct lack of with-you-ness between the horse and rider. Rather, the horse has his mind elsewhere—probably back at the barn with his buddies in this scenario—and therefore, trouble is brewing.

So many people try to fix this problem mechanically. Changing bits, thinking that a harsher bit will give a person more control, is often thought to be an answer. That hardly relieves the problem, though. It might give more control to the rider in a sense that a more painful bit might make the horse more reluctant to be disobedient, but it is hardly likely to relieve even an ounce of the tension in the horse. Most likely, it will increase the horse's discomfort and desire to go to somewhere else where he has freedom and comfort.

Or, for another example, it is not uncommon to see tack used to tie down a horse's head when being ridden. Why is a horse's head high in the first place? A tense horse usually raises his head and gets quite "upside-down." Does tying down the head fix the problem? Well, the horse may be physically unable to raise his head when it is tied down, but that certainly does not change the horse's desire to raise his head in his tension. Very likely such a horse is bracing hard against that tie-down strap just as hopeful to get elsewhere as he ever was.

Humans tend to go after treating the symptoms of horse troubles rather than working to eliminate the disease that causes them in the first place. The main disease in nearly every case of horse trouble we come across is rooted in horses holding onto other thoughts rather than letting go of them to be present with a person, and thus being willing to think and act with a person to perform a task.

My experiences and the many examples I have seen from Harry's clinics over the years are completely convincing on this matter. If we are talking about horsemanship theory and philosophy, getting a horse's thought is the very foundation of the means of understanding how to have a more relaxed, willing partner in a horse. If we want to talk application of effective horsemanship, it boils down to using ways to get the horse's mind with us that have the practical result of a softer more focused horse.

If we are having troubles with a horse, we do well to ask ourselves, "Where is this horse's mind at this moment." Follow that up with, "How can I get his mind with me here?" and we are on the trail to reducing that horse's troubles.

CHAPTER FIFTEEN

Interest and Imagination

Saturday, 16 May 2015—Mendin' Fences Farm, Rogersville, Tennessee.

"That's the kind of interest and look that will take you someplace someday," Harry shared.

I like that Harry's quote above links the work done with a horse in clinic (training) settings to eventually using a horse out in the "real world." It reminds me that the work of improving ones horsemanship, while wonderful and fulfilling in and of itself, is pointing forward to making practical applications with a willing horse. To top it off, the quote gives a helpful clue of what to look for in our training work that can provide great benefits in the future when we take a horse out of the confines of the training pen.

Harry's remark makes me think about straightness in a horse. We can work on straightening a crooked horse by tipping the horse's head this way and moving a shoulder that way—you know, helping the horse to get straight. And that kind of work can be beneficial at times. But Harry helped me to understand that (as in the last chapter where treating symptoms versus tackling the disease that causes them was discussed) if a horse has an interest in going someplace, he tends to line himself out straight and go there.

In other words, if you get a horse interested in going

someplace, he gets straight because that is how an interested horse goes to interesting places.

Yet another simple idea, right? But then comes the follow-up question, so how do you get a horse interested in going somewhere?

I have been rather fascinated over the years to observe Harry's uncanny ability to get a horse interested in doing things in empty arenas and round pens. I will go so far as to say Harry gets a horse as interested in going and doing things in these rather dull, empty places as he does out in the wide, wild, world outside of the pen—so I know it can be done. I have gotten a mental grip on this lesson, and gotten a lot better at it over the years, too. The key to success with getting a horse interested in doing something with a person in large part is the person's own interest and imagination.

It's not hard to realize that trotting endless circles, for example, is just not all that interesting for horses. I can't remember ever driving past a pasture and looking over to see a horse just out there on his own trotting a bunch of circles for fun. Add to that a human imposed routine to the training work, and you've really got a recipe for a drilled horse who wants to be free from it. We certainly can set a horse up to want to take his mind elsewhere to avoid dying from boredom.

I have heard Harry address this point at clinics. He has suggested people do things like imagine a cow to work in the pen with them, or imagine a line on the ground to be followed, or any number of things. And the key is for the person to add an element of importance to whatever is being done with the horse so that the horse picks up on it. Everything that we ask of our horses should be presented as important enough to the horse to take notice and get with us. Otherwise, why would we go to the trouble of asking it? When a request is not made to be important, the horse is learning that what we ask can be ignored—and that's not a helpful reality when it is time to go and do something with a horse.

I rode a horse for a client one time that pops to mind

when I think about this topic. The horse was a big 17 hand-ish warmblood; a Dressage horse, who recently had come back from a year and a half of training with some issues. As this particular session started, the owner was riding the horse. Tension was building in the horse and the client, and things weren't going very well. Then at a walk to trot transition, the horse bucked. She rode it okay and then dismounted, handed me the reins, and said, "Here!"

I had seen how the horse was ridden in the arena a few times. Uninteresting lines down the fence and a few circles here and there, always ridden with a great deal of contact. The horse looked longingly out to the side as if to say, "Boy, I'd rather be over there away from this."

I took the reins and moved the horse around a little from the ground to be certain he wasn't about to bust before I climbed on top of the skyscraper. He seemed okay enough, so up I went into the saddle. I kept slack in the reins and asked him to move forward. He stepped out fine but then I felt some tension building, so I picked up one rein and turned him and released when he thought in that direction. We went forward a few steps, then I picked up the other rein, waited for his thought to come through in that direction, and released to a full slack rein going forward again. The tension seemed to fade a bit. Then I looked around me and noticed signs with letters at different points along the arena fence.

Ding!

I got the idea that we needed to get to E.

I mean that we REALLY needed to get to E, like our lives depended on it. I brought up a sudden urgency in me and focused on getting to E like there was a hot lasagna waiting for me there.

The horse delayed, unaccustomed to such an urgent request (indeed any request outside of the usual arena stuff was a real mind-blower that he was unprepared for), but then he picked up on the feel I was presenting and took off at a big trot for E.

It reminded me of how in a herd sometimes one horse gets

ahold of something in the environment and moves out towards it and the others pick up on that and move along too, though not necessarily knowing what or why. The feel from one horse going intently sometimes is all the motivation that the others need to take a real interest and follow. That is the kind of shared interest that "takes you someplace."

Right before we got to the fence at E, I stopped (in my body) and gave a slight suggestion on what had been totally slack reins that he think about stopping. Well, he mostly didn't.

In retrospect, I think the horse was so accustomed to being ridden with tight contact and working to ignore the rider that what I offered simply lacked importance to him. It was like riding a locomotive. He thus wasn't really focused on me, on what was going on around him, or on the big white fence in front of him—he was just chugging right on down the tracks. Even though he had picked up on the urgency I suggested about going to E, his mind was mostly elsewhere when we got there.

He hit the letter E and the fence where the letter sign hung with his chest so hard that the fence groaned and nearly toppled. I had a hunch that the client might not be very impressed with my amazing horsemanship skills at that moment. But rather than worry about it, I kept on with my quickly evolving plan.

I picked up the right rein, and with all the urgency of a third grader heading for recess I spun the warmblood around and headed for M like my hair was on fire and that's where a pail of water was waiting.

Off we went to M. The horse was stupefied at first, clearly not accustomed to being asked anything important or outside of the regular routine in an arena—and never given a slack rein to go forward. I had his attention now.

Already, after the fence crashing ordeal, he felt way more with me even though the reins were completely slack as I rode him. It was a great instance showing that contact on the reins was not the answer to having a horse like this listen. But rather having his mind on task and getting some importance in the task at hand clearly made the difference.

As we approached M, I quit the go in my body and barely touched the reins. We stopped squarely in front of M pretty as you please.

I rubbed the horse's neck and gave him a moment to be still there and soak on things. This also was a great example of letting a horse take some responsibility in the relationship. Yes, at E and M I had communicated lightly with my body and the reins that he should be aware and stop, but I did not make him do it. When he remained distracted and smashed into the fence at E, he discovered that there were consequences for being distracted when I rode him—that I was not going to micro-manage every little bit of all that we did together. It's pretty obvious that other riders he had experience with had not allowed him the freedom to smash into a fence (go figure). But now that he had a crazy person on his back to deal with, he quickly learned that he'd better pay attention as he might have to help this idiot avoid some serious wrecks.

Then I upped my energy and off we went back to E like we were packing gold in the saddlebags and being chased by banditos. This time at E he heard me just fine and he stopped and stood with ease by the big black letter hanging on the slightly bowed-out fence. He was perfectly quiet as he stood there, although he had begun to breathe and I noticed his large frame heave a bit with each breath; he must have been holding his breath in his tension before and was letting down a bit now. No busy mouth or jittery movements showed up as they had earlier. It was a very nice change, and the horse felt completely different than he had only a few minutes before.

I kept up the game for another couple of letters and then began to ride him around the arena, throwing in a few leg yields and circles here and there to feel how this big horse could move. What a difference that game had made in getting him mentally onto tasks with me.

It is important to consider that the difference was not caused by the "exercise" of specifically what I had asked him to do. Chasing the alphabet around the arena wasn't a silver bullet in itself. The new found relaxation and willingness in this horse was a direct result of getting him interested in what was going on, so his mind was focused with me on the tasks at hand and he really participated in them.

So, to revisit the quote...Harry said, "*That's the kind of interest and look that will take you someplace someday.*" The above is an example of getting the kind of interest that will take you someplace, but what does it look like?

If you spend much time around horses, especially around a herd of horses in some open pasture, you should not have to wait very long before you witness a horse getting an interest and going somewhere. The eyes and ears are typically pointed in the direction of interest as it is the horse's primary thought at that moment. There is a kind of commitment visible in the body—a balance and readiness, then a movement—that shows the horse is planning to go somewhere and then goes...a straightness in his body.

Whether it be in ground work or riding, in the confines of an arena or out in the world, it is helpful to notice these kinds of interested actions in a horse so they may be sought after in our horsemanship. If a person goes to ride towards E in an arena and the horse's head is up high and tipped off to one side, his ears are penned, and/or he doesn't walk with an effort, that's a pretty sure bet he is not interested in going to E.

The example above is one instance used to address bringing interest to an empty arena. Looking at it circles us back to the discussion of imagination on the part of the person. A child may look out into his back yard and see cowboys and Indians lurking about, or tigers peering out from the hedge, or a swing may become a parachute and provide great adventure as the child jumps from an airplane and swings along as he heads towards the earth. As adults, we seem to become less imaginative and see only a rusty swing set and bushes around that need to be trimmed. But there is no reason we can't apply ourselves to get more imaginative with our horses.

One thing to do is to set up some obstacles or other gear, like a pedestal or mailbox, to provide interesting activities to do with horses. I've seen whole playgrounds set up for horse work—Harry had a very extensive one at his place in Arizona, and I saw a humdinger of a playground at one of his clinic in Montana. These can have bridges, "car washes" made from foam noodles, pits full of empty plastic bottles, and even see-saws for people and horses to teeter-totter on. But honestly, even opening a gate or riding from one post to another across a pasture can be a great way for the person and horse to gain focus with nothing fancy in the environment.

As interest inducing as some props can be for horses, the real benefit about using these things is to get the human really focused and operating the horse in a very clear, particular way. Then the horse picks up on the human's focus and intent. To be honest, I have seen horses come through during some playground work as if to say, "Finally, you've offered something for me to go with!"

Horsemanship is all about a horse feeling of us and us feeling of a horse. A distracted horse is not a horse picking up on an interest that we would like for him to have. An interested horse who is straight between the reins and taking us someplace has a certain sublime feeling about it—a real togetherness. Noticing what these both look and feel like, and playing with how to get the better parts, can make a huge difference in getting us thinking about how to better bring the positives to the relationship.

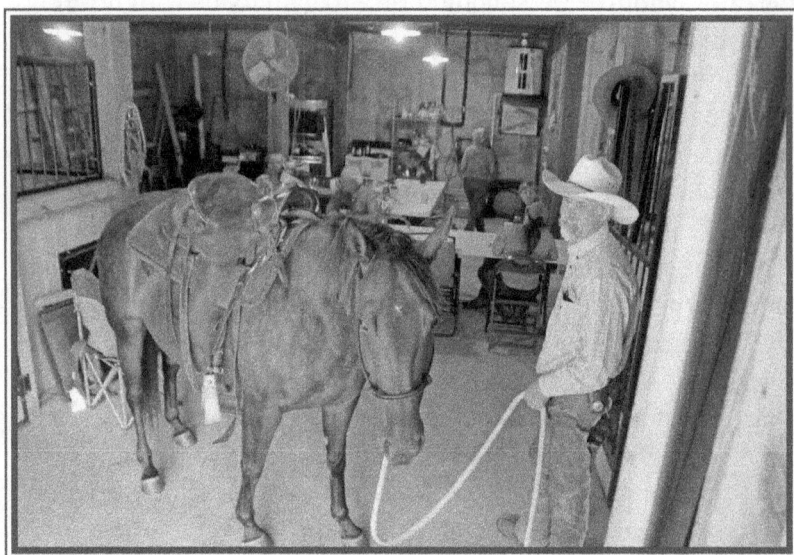

Over the decade and a half we've hosted the Harry Whitney/Ronnie Moyer Bible/horsemanship clinics here in Virginia, we've been set up in a lot of different kinds of places to pull it off. And more than once we've had our meals in a barn. Here's Mirage and me with some other folks in the dining room! (Photo: Harry Whitney)

CHAPTER SIXTEEN
The First Search Day

Friday, May 12, 2023—inaugural clinic Search Day held at Mendin' Fences Farm in Rogersville, Tennessee.

"I didn't try to make something be; I just didn't let it work out so she tried something different." I jotted this quote down in my notebook as Harry spoke the words during the very first Search Day at Mendin' Fences Farm.

Over the years, Harry has played with setting up deliberate searches for horses during clinics. Many folks have come to call these "free searches" because they often are conducted with horses at liberty. Setting up searches with horses is a topic that is vast, and setting up deliberate searches in clinic settings seems to be a unique kind of project pioneered by Harry. Others have taken the idea and worked with it, too—most notably clinician Libby Lyman, who spent a lot of time at Harry's place in Salome, Arizona and explored horse searches to great lengths. I had the pleasure of talking to Libby about her free search experiences on several occasions and shared some of those conversations in Chapter Nine of the book, *Further Along the Trail*.

Harry's interest in setting up searches for horses is in part for the horse to have a chance to work through some scenarios on his own without real directing from a person. This brings up some interesting choices and behaviors in horses, and horses who have had very little opportunity to explore their options when interacting with people, like those who have been severely micro-managed in their training and work like the Warmblood from the example in the last chapter, can show quite a range of actions and sometimes see some benefits from the experience. But the main reason Harry developed the searches, he says, is for people to see and better understand what horses really go through when given the opportunity to have real freedom within a certain space to explore their options.

One large part of what's at play in these searches, Harry explains, is that people have a very difficult time not directing a horse to do something. This is true even when he instructs them not to, and they try not to. In the search, either Harry or another person will be in some proximity to the horse and do some action occasionally to keep a horse searching. Often, this amounts to something like having the person sit in a chair facing one direction and flapping a flag on the ground. The flag flapping is handled by whacking the flag on the ground in the same spot each time, for example. The flag is not used to indicate direction or other movements specifically—rather, it is just used to motivate the horse to begin searching for something, anything, new to try when he gets "stuck."

The unique set-up search is a big and non-typical horsemanship topic to grapple with. Perhaps the best way to share this idea is to describe one of the searches from the first official Search Day that the above quote came from to help show what one looks like.

Harry's quote, "*I didn't try to make something be; I just didn't let it work out so she tried something different*," shares the essence of the kind of horse search that he worked to demonstrate that day. Namely, that Harry did not try to direct the horse to do something specific during each search even though there were specific tasks set up ahead of time for each of the three horses to achieve.

That may sound a bit contradictory.... A trio of photos accompanies this chapter taken during the search Harry did with

Gomer, a 2,000 pound, 18:1 hand Percheron gelding owned by Katie Mills from Vermont, that I hope help to explain the art of the search as demonstrated by Harry.

In general, Harry merely made a move flapping a flag in the same spot and in the same way while sitting in a chair some distance from the horse. It was plain to see that there was no specific directing to his flagging to indicate to Gomer that the gelding should do something in particular. Rather, the flag just indicated that whatever the gelding was trying at a given point was not the answer and to keep searching for something else. Various positions and motions that the horse tried over time got crossed off his list because of the recurring flapping flag. The flagging also prompted Gomer to try some new things until eventually, Bingo! He hit on the very thing Harry was looking for. The process took some time and I will explain it in greater detail with reference to the photos below.

It can be strong in a person to want to help lead the horse directly to what is wanted, and that reveals how strong it can be in us humans to want to make the horse do something rather than let the horse work through it for himself. And the list of other things the horse tries before arriving at the desired thing can be very long—hours long, sometimes.

Photo 1 shows us Gomer in his first favorite position: hanging out at the side of the arena by the gate that is in the direction of the stalls where the other horses were kept down a hill. Notice Harry sitting in a chair with a flag on the ground by his right leg. Harry occasionally flapped the flag right there on the ground—but nowhere else. This proved enough disturbance to encourage Gomer to explore new things in the pen. You can see that there are three panels in front of Harry set up in a triangle. This arrangement produced a small alleyway between the arena fence and one panel of the triangle. The goal for this search was to see if Harry could get Gomer voluntarily to pass through the space between the fence and the triangle panel, and it was a pretty tight squeeze for the big fella.

Photo 2 depicts a big change in Gomer's try choices. For

Photo 1

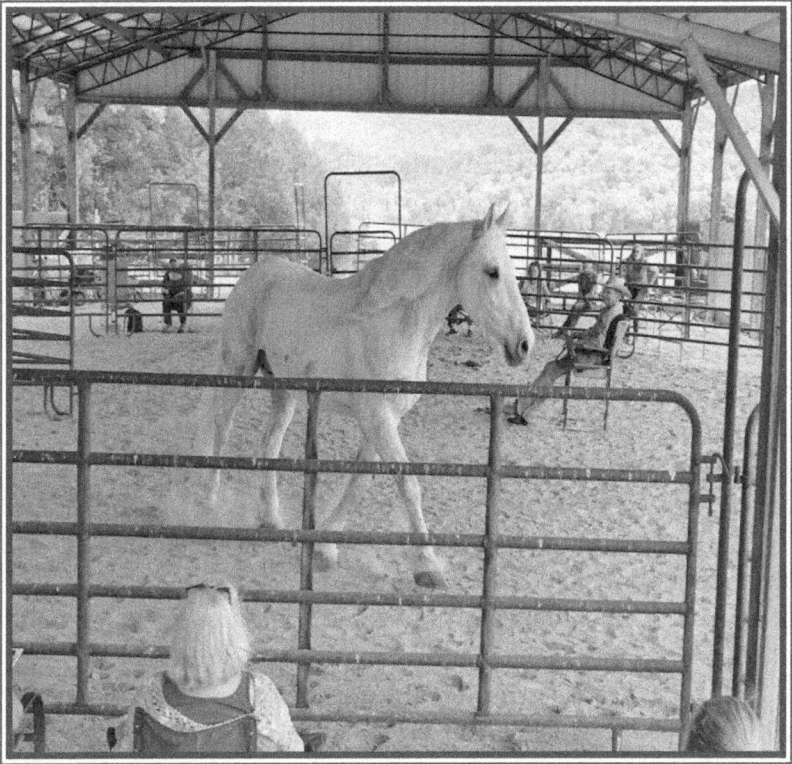

Photo 2

more than an hour, Gomer mostly made variations of a clockwise circle in the area to Harry's right by the gate, and very occasionally the gelding would make a rushed pass behind Harry's chair and then back to his favorite area. Harry flagged at times to indicate that those things weren't working out. It was not a constant flagging, but rather the flagging was timed to give Gomer the chance to try things, even the same things, for awhile—and he had plenty of opportunity to stop and look at Harry and see if this or that was going to be the answer. When Harry flagged (as stated earlier, always flagging in the same spot by his right leg and in the same way, while sitting in the chair to be non-directive), the gelding would go on the move, again searching.

Many times Gomer came back to try the same spot again as if to say, "Are you SURE this isn't it? I really think it ought to be!" When Gomer tried something new—like going counterclockwise in the same area for a change and then stopped, Harry often gave him more time before flagging. I think this encouraged the horse to try new things. But before long, the flag engaged again and it was time to try something else since Gomer still was not showing any signs of considering squeezing through the tight panel space.

As a back-story note, upon arriving at Mendin' Fences Farm for the clinic, Gomer displayed concern about gates in general and rushed through them and through any tight spaces. That was part of the reason that Harry came up with the idea to set up the tight-ish space between the panels as a search for him.

In this second photo, Gomer has made his biggest change yet and has not only begun to try going counterclockwise, but is in the side of the pen to Harry's left—and it was more than an hour of searching before he tried this innovation.

Photo 3 speaks for itself! Yay Gomer! We all were delighted when the big gelding figured out for himself to put going through that tight space between the panels on his menu of options. In fact, many people expressed amazement that the gelding ever would try such a thing as going through that tight space on his own because it so obviously was not a place the horse would want to go seemingly without some form of direct prompting from a person. And that's one great reason Harry does these searches—to prove to people what lengths a horse will go to have harmony in his world. And that making things happen with them by default is not the best way to get a horse to come along with our ideas.

It took an 1 hour and 45 minutes of searching for Gomer to hit pay dirt. Harry pointed out that this kind of grand, overt search is meant to demonstrate the process that a horse goes through when given the chance to come to conclusions on his own rather than being made to do something by the human. And that this kind of search can be presented by the human in

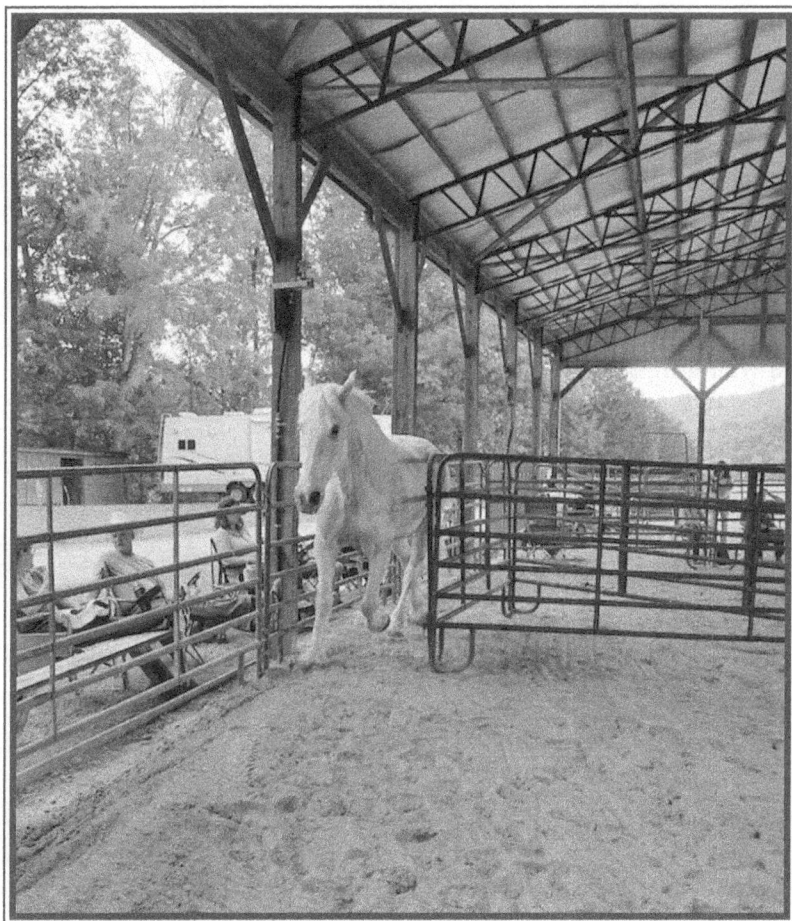

Photo 3

much that we undertake with horses. It even can be applied to such tiny moves as engaging a rein, asking something with the lead rope, or nearly any other request we make of our horses. Harry remarked that we can present requests in a similar way to allow horses to try a variety of things and mark them off the lists themselves until they find the "answer," and that this profoundly changes the way they feel about coming along with the human. Rather than the pinched up, icky feelings that often accompany driving horses into motions and making them do things, they can be provided the opportunity to search out things for themselves and feel they had a choice in the matter. And that the choice they made works out better than anything else.

It's really something to behold; as Harry said in another search on that day, "*I didn't try to make something be; I just didn't let it work out so she tried something different.*" Observing all that a horse will go through to arrive at a choice on his own that is hoped for by the human really can change our perspective of how to approach many requests we make of a horse. And while I sat watching Harry with rapt attention during the three searches that day, watching Harry sit in a chair and do nothing for long stretches of time may not be for everybody!

CHAPTER SEVENTEEN

Preserving the Search

Sunday, May 28, 2023—second clinic Search Day held at Mendin' Fences Farm in Rogersville, Tennessee.

"People criticize a search in a foal who is full of search and drive it out of him. But, you can get things working without it feeling like a criticism. You can discourage the behavior in an encouraging way." Harry said this during one of the searches on the second Search Day.

This chapter's opening quote from Harry, for me, at least, carries plenty of gravity. And I realize that this quote is quite similar to the one from Chapter Four. But it is such an important point that it is worth revisiting and considering from many angles.

Starting young horses is a singularly significant undertaking, one that comes with a ton of responsibility. If you have been around Harry much, you'll be familiar with one of Harry's favorite sayings (also previously mentioned in Chapter Four), "So they're started, so they go."

That statement is so true. Adult horse problems often are traceable back to early experiences between humans and horses.

So...just a little pressure on us humans to get it right with the youngsters, eh?

At the same time, approaching young, inexperienced horses with patience and some good horsemanship skills to get things going well right from the start is amazingly fun and fulfilling. It is thrilling to offer a new request to a young horse and experience that youngster figure it out and follow it through with relaxation. And to watch confidence build with these kinds of interactions. Such an approach should provide a lifetime of positive relationships between horses and humans.

This chapter's quote points out that foals typically pop into the world full of curiosity. What a gift it is to us that horses enter the world looking for answers and information, and even can show curiosity about us humans and what we might want to do with them. If this is true, then how is it that people don't take full advantage of such a wonderful quality for the horses' benefit when training them? This question leads to another part of Harry's quote, that we can drive the search out of them.

It seems it is deep in human nature to drive horses around to make them do things rather than to ask them to see if we can get communication and willingness working. One can assume, or at least hope, that this unhappy result derives from people just not knowing any better. People newly exposed to Harry's kind of horsemanship often are astonished when they observe things like a horse looking in a direction and then walking off that way just because a person provided some feel on a slack lead rope without any driving. There seems to be a default setting in humans that says: the only way to get a horse to do something is to drive the horse to do it.

The previous chapter discusses horse searches and provides the example of Gomer's search from Harry's first official Search Day in Tennessee. This example shines a light on how horses can find the answers we want them to when they are provided an opportunity to explore their options and then come to conclusions on their own.

If we again take up the example of Harry and Gomer but this time turn it upside down, then we can look honestly at how things typically might go with a human trying to get a gelding to squeeze between the arena fence and a panel. The person begins by driving the horse towards one opening and then keeps the pressure on him. Gomer, in this reverse scenario, would be blocked hard from trying to turn around to escape the opening between the panels or trying anything else. Continual pressure would be placed on the boxed-in horse to attempt to force him to squeeze his body between the panels regardless of what he thought or felt about the situation. As a result, the horse might go through the opening much more quickly than the extensive time it took for Harry to work it out giving Gomer lots of time to search. This driving pressure approach, however, also might end up in a big fat wreck.

Whether the horse goes through the space quickly or a wreck or some other scenario results, it is easy to understand how a horse would feel fear, confinement, and a definite lack of options in that predicament. And since the human obviously is the one boxing-in the horse, the horse rightly associates the person with this turmoil. That ill feeling can stick with a horse and carry across many aspects of his relationships with humans. And if this is an early, formative experience with people, it takes very little imagination to perceive how such behavior can taint a horse's perceptions towards humans as being untrustworthy and dangerous creatures.

"So they're started; so they go!"

Such not-so-great interactions with people working to force horses to do what is wanted also can teach horses that using their innate curiosity gets them into trouble with humans—that searching for answers is a bad thing. Horses at first tend to try and figure out what works best with people, and horses are likely to be very curious about these two-legged creatures who want to interact with them. But humans can at worst punish horses for this, or at least, by continuing a pressure campaign to get them to do what the person wants, cause horses to conclude that their own input of searching for answers in the situation simply does not work out. Under such pressures as in our reverse example with Gomer above, horses often learn to try and get by mechanically, acquiescing with their bodies to what is asked and shutting down their minds or looking for distractions to displace their worried thoughts in the process. Or sometimes in extreme cases, they just try to take out the human as a way to get rid of this problem.

Often, such a scenario causes confusion in horses as they honestly may have no clue what the person is asking even though the person thinks it should be perfectly obvious. Or, perhaps it is understood what the person wants, but it is a terrifying request for the horse, especially if no time is allowed for the horse to check things out to make sure it is safe. Adding any inconsistency to how people ask a horse to do something intensifies a horse's worry, and worries can bring about unwanted behaviors.

Going back to the opening quote, let's turn attention to the final part of it and look at how one discourages behaviors in horses in an encouraging way.

One of the ways this works out is by the human having a specific goal in mind when discouraging a behavior. In other words, one behavior is discouraged but because there is another one in mind that we know will work out very well for the horse and the human, we leave the door wide open for the search towards that positive new thing to take place. There's a freedom offered for the horse to explore his options even though we may discourage "incorrect" things that the horse gets stuck on—yet, we don't make them horrible or impossible. If the horse is pretty stuck on a distraction, it may take some pretty biggish activity to get him to let that go and try something else. But when handled well, the horse doesn't feel driven away from us and into something else but rather feels encouraged to try something besides the thing where he is stuck.

This may sound like splitting hairs, but there is a big difference in the feel between driving a horse—an action that by its very nature means the pressure is such that the horse also is getting away from the person—and encouraging a change of thought (and that change of thought is to go with what we are wanting to do).

We need look no further than the search with Gomer from the previous chapter to have a great example of this. Gomer was discouraged from standing at the gate and looking down the hill where his horse buddies were stalled by Harry flapping the flag. Later, he was discouraged from making circles behind Harry's chair in the same way. But to achieve these discouragements, Harry did not make them impossible for Gomer but rather Harry only had to flap his flag on the ground beside the chair where he sat to indicate that those things probably weren't working out. This really is equally an encouragement to try something else as it is a discouragement to stop being stuck on the thing that Harry didn't want to work out.

Another good example is trailer loading. If you've ever seen a person or people together try to make a horse get into a trailer, you can no-doubt attest to how horrifying an experience that can be for a horse. But, if a person spends some time at the back of an open trailer working to not let being outside the trailer work out so well and then allowing the horse to try thinking about inside the trailer for himself and letting that work out great, with any luck, that horse works out for himself trying to get into the trailer. But working to drive one into a trailer...well that puts a whole different feel to the situation. It can amp up the horse's worry, and fear will trump curiosity. Once the horse knows he's being boxed-in rather than exploring his options, well, that often gets the horse working harder against the task of going into the trailer and can confirm in the horse's mind that the trailer a scary place for any future loadings, too.

Not being emotional when asking a horse to do something pops to mind as a helpful tool when preserving a horse's curiosity and getting willing responses. Anger is a really big concern here because people can get angry pretty fast if a horse doesn't do what they want when they want, and anger certainly brings up fear and confusion in horses. And anger can cause people to do regrettable things. But, any emotionality in the human's ask can spike a horse's concern. Human emotions like apprehension, fear, or even seemingly positive ones like adulation spilling out when people work with horses can be a source of worry for horses. Horses can perceive human emotional reactions as the person acting oddly, often out-of-the-blue, and that can smack of unpredictability and add fuel to a horse's lack of togetherness with a person.

And I guess I should muddy the waters here a bit and mentioned the well timed fit that is a great, helpful horsemanship tool. The fit (or any getting big enough to get a horses attention, whatever that might look like) is helpful primarily when it is done in a matter-of-fact and non-emotional way, and is well timed to discourage the horse from having his mind distracted and is not used to drive the horse into something.

There's plenty to this topic that can keep a person thinking. I'll just wrap up by saying that this topic makes me think about how horses are very much in the moment. It seems that people often do not realize just how close to the surface the horse's hard-wired self preservation instincts are. If we understand that horses can have life-or-death worries even at home in their own regular environments when we ask something of them, that understanding can go a long way towards handling how we approach them. A horse's natural curiosity gets washed over with fear when situations arise that are worrisome. Considering this fact can be a great tool in the horsemanship toolbox to help guide our approaches and always look with care to see that we encourage horses to search and avoid driving them into things.

CHAPTER EIGHTEEN

Being Here First

Sunday, May 8, 2022—First Day of the First Intensive clinic for the season at Mendin' Fences Farm in Rogersville, Tennessee.

"Few horses I meet are familiar with first being here. He's thinking everywhere but here. He's thinking how good it is out there somewhere. The more they don't want to be here the more important those things [out there] become," Harry said.

A Friesian/Quarter Horse cross gelding has kept things interesting for me over the past few weeks. The tall, lanky, bay horse recently was purchased by existing clients of mine and they called me in to help because he presented as pushy and hard to catch. As is not particularly unusual, his previous owner called him a broke trail horse, and there was video of him being ridden and looking fabulous on the trail, of course. At his new home, however, he was very herd bound, particularly to one of the mares, and the new owners needed some help figuring out just what was going on with the newcomer and if he was indeed rideable.

The first time I went out to work him, the owner was not able to catch him. Perhaps my presence had him on high alert not helping matters, but for whatever reason, it took her an hour to get the halter on the gelding. Once caught, I was able to lead him out of his home pasture and over to a larger-than-most round pen and away from the rest of the herd. The walk itself was a bit of a challenge at first as the rascal was pining for his friend and, yes, he proved to be pushy. I began calling him the llama-horse because of the extremely high head he carried due to the serious tension that often welled up in him. I stopped and backed him many times along the way, getting his mind a bit more with me and seeing how that in turn brought some softness into the creature and even caused his llama head posture to lower at times.

The trip across a yard and part of another pasture to the round pen worked out okay. Once in the pen, I turned the gelding loose to let him move around a bit and see if it was possible to establish a connection between us. I got my flag and a rope halter and lead rope and stood in the center of the pen.

If nothing else, the situation that unfolded with this fella provides the perfect example to discuss this chapter's Harry quote. The gelding was anything but familiar with being "here." Those thoughts of his were everywhere but "here" in that pen. As these kind of cases go, he was a pretty severe case of mind-gone-outa-the-pen.

At first, oddly enough, the horse, who was probably 16 hands, would stop as I approached and he would bow up his back like one of those Halloween cats you see drawings of, and then he'd just about bust before I could touch him. When I did touch him, he'd relax a bit. I managed to get in a few of those approaches with him standing still and touch him. But once he realized that I was giving him the freedom to search me up in the round pen (or not), he made his choice—the choice not to stop and let me approach him anymore. And forget about him approaching me!

The horse got to pounding those hooves of his out by the panels, always keeping track of the other horses way up the hill when he could get his eyes on them. He also looked hard in other directions when circling the pen at a herd of goats on another place up the road or for a barking dog a quarter mile away. Anything seemed better than thinking about being in the pen with me.

This basic scenario is a familiar one and has played out with horses and me plenty of times before, so I was hopeful that my acquired skills would get this deal turned around for the better pretty quickly. The gelding's preferred stopping spot became the panel closest in the direction of his herd mates where he would place his head over the top of the panel and look intensely at the other horses. When he was there, or even passing by that spot, I flagged a good kerwhack on the ground. Often when this situation is set up, after a few trips around the pen getting kerwhacks at that spot, the horse anticipates the coming kerwhack and will stop ahead of that spot and look me up to keep the kerwhack from happening. Not this fella. Nope. He just kept right on going around looking like a llama causing predictable kerwhacks in the same place each time.

So I resorted to plan 1.2 and I stepped a little closer to the panel at the spot where the flagging occurred as he passed it. This little bit of squeeze adds significance to the foreseeable kerwhacks and often gets a tough case horse to stop and look me up. Not this guy. He kept on rushing right past there like he didn't even notice me.

This brings us back to Harry's quote up top. *"The more they don't want to be here the more important those things [out there] become."* I stood there watching him lathering up with sweat and thinking to myself, he REALLY doesn't want to be here if he is that dedicated to his distractions! And here's a horse who has no history with me personally, but for all of his previous handling, training, and trail riding experiences with others, he certainly had a strong, opinion about me (the human in general)—and it wasn't good if he was that eager to take his mind out of the pen.

The first time I worked him in the round pen, we did manage to get to a somewhat better spot but mainly after I managed to block him pretty hard and convince him to stop and let me approach him. That's when I got the halter back on him and did some ground work on line. Part of that session involved leading him back out of the round pen gate and through two other gates to his beloved herd. It involved a bunch of backing—backing him off of me as I opened the gates, backing him up as I went out, and asking him to stop before stepping all the way through the gate and then getting him to back up and let go of that forward push before I let him come all the way through. That all went remarkably well considering how rough the liberty work had looked.

A few days later, I returned for round two.

Luckily, we had agreed for the owners to have the fella already in the round pen when I arrived, and he was. I later heard that this was accomplished by leading his equine girlfriend into the round pen, whom he readily followed in, and then removing her and leaving him.

I entered the round pen with my flag and a rope halter with a lead rope, went to the center of the pen, and began working the gelding as I had the previous session—flagging as he passed a certain spot or two to see if I could get him to let go of those distractions out there and bring his mind back into the pen and to me. If "*the more they don't want to be here the more important those things [out there] become,*" then I clearly could see that his desire not to be with me had increased considerably since the time before because those horses out there were an even stronger distraction this time.

Of course, it would be great to report that my remarkable horsemanship skills had this session looking ever-so-much better after the worried Friesian/Quarter Horse cross had soaked on our previous session, but the opposite was true. The gelding proved to be really amped up and hard-focused on those other horses, goats, chickens, and whatever else he could find out there. The llama-horse seemed even more frustrated and rushy than before. There was one change I had been able to get the first session that had stuck, and I took some solace in it.

The horse clearly had gotten the memo that bringing his mind and body towards me was the idea because when he turned to change direction, now he turned towards me rather than away from me and would step in such a way that it seemed like he was going to walk right up to me. But each time as I got excited seeing this behavior, my hopes were dashed as he did a drive-by and off he went around the pen again. But it was something to show that he seemed to be getting warmer.

Even though that little bit of progress had stuck, the second session otherwise appeared worse than the first. The horse allowed me to approach and pet him, bowing up again like a hissing cat, once right at the beginning, but no more. He went and went and went around that pen with his head tilted outside and looking hard out there at everything and nothing.

I have a theory about this.

I think what occurred was that the gelding, increasingly understanding that he had the freedom to explore his options, was taking full advantage of it, probably for the first time in his life as related to humans. When a horse has been boxed in and made to do everything with the options severely curtailed in the training, a horse can just shut down mentally and go through the motions the best he can. Open up that door, and they can show that they feel pretty lousy about humans when you get right down to it.

Had the gelding felt comforted by my presence and was either curious or trusting in me, these sessions would have looked way different. The horse would have started to look me up and probably tried coming up to check me out. But there was none of that. The horse had full knowledge of what the human was about (in his experience), and it wasn't particularly good. So my job now was to convince him that his experiences were wrong—and for the horse who is at his core an experiential learner, that can be a tough job!

That second session put me into a bit of a dilemma. I'm not one to leave off working with a horse in a bad spot. I am convinced that leaves him returning the next time a person goes to work with him with increased anxiety and turmoil, and can set the next go off on the wrong hoof. But now I had a horse who was lathered up in sweat and whipping around out there along the panels of this larger than usual round pen and I couldn't get near enough to him to get a halter on or intervene and help him settle and find a better spot. I did have my lariat, so I grabbed it, built a loop, and after a few minutes of swinging the rope around to see if perhaps that might help to get his mind more centered on me (it did not), I roped him.

Once roped, he knew he was caught, but his mind still was gone way out there. *"The more they don't want to be here the more important those things [out there] become,"* continued to prove true even once he was roped. The rope was further down his neck close to his shoulders than I had wanted it to be, providing me less influence over his head and making it pretty difficult (let's call it impossible) to get him bent and stopped as I worked to put on the brakes. And his massive, flowy, Fresiany mane got all wrapped in the loop so the job of moving it up the neck towards his head was complicated even further. Persistence paid off, and I finally got him stopped by walking along side of him and pretending that I was leading him even though there was five feet between us, and he believed it. I used that opportunity to reel him in closer and closer until I was petting him and stopped him. As he was heaving getting his breath caught up and looking again like a llama with bug eyes, I untangled the lariat and got the loop situated at the top of his neck by his jaw.

I petted him and assured him that he wasn't in any trouble. Then I used the lariat as if it were a normal halter/lead rope combination. I often do this when working horses. I enjoy letting the horses feel a different and freer connection on their heads, and when demonstrating this to folks it often surprises them that the horse can feel the offers and get on board with what is being asked just like with a halter with only the rope around their necks.

This went really well, and in no time he was circling me

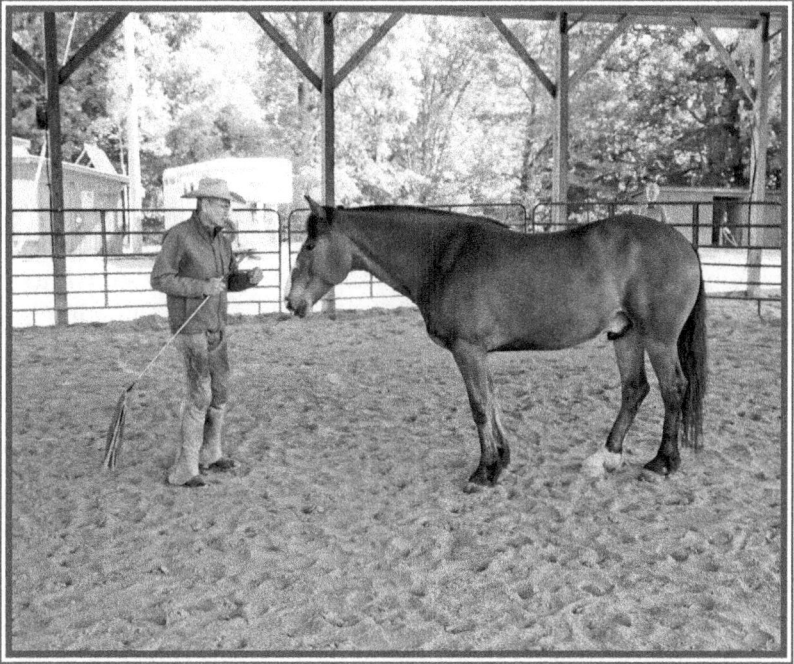

Harry has some success getting Bay's mind "here" as he begins the opening session on May 13, 2023, the first day of the second Intensive Clinic that year at Mendin' Fences Farm in Rogersville, Tennessee.

both directions, backing up, coming to me—and it looked just like it would have with the halter and lead rope. The gelding was following along okay, so knowing that he was caught did a lot towards convincing him to let go of the worst of that distractedness.

A good, relaxed spot came along with the lariat ground work and I took the opportunity to switch to the halter and lead rope and then led the critter out of the round pen and let him free to roam the pasture with his horse buddies.

I was not at all satisfied with what had take place. First of all, there had not been a shift for the better when he was at liberty, so in my mind there was no real improvement in the relationship between us when he had more freedom. He merely conformed when he was caught, and although that did allow me to get my hands on him and get him settled and more with me, that was not nearly the level of okayness I wanted.

Secondly, it was clear that as rough as this was going in the round pen with me, the owners were going to struggle even more than I did. Supporting this horse to a better spot seemed like a very tough job and I was left wondering if the llama-horse was a horse that they could deal with reasonably, let alone if he would provide any kind of hope for them to have a riding horse.

Over the next few days I spent plenty of time rehashing the most recent and challenging session with the Friesian/Quarter Horse gelding in my head. I wondered if this horse was experiencing a burst of very strong effort to try other the things right before a breakthrough to go with what the human is offering him to do. It's a situation I have heard Harry discuss at clinics. Trailer loading is one place this shows up in spades. Just when you think the horse is about to drop his head and walk into the trailer, BAM!, off he goes in the opposite direction with redoubled effort and hits the end of the rope and has a fit! Two minutes later, with a little more persistence, on walks the horse, completely thinking up into the trailer as he goes willingly and seemingly finally fully satisfied that he has exhausted all of the other possibilities available to him. Whew!

The situation in the round pen, however, did not appear that way to me. It seemed more like the gelding was fully committed to his distractions. That he might go all week long without turning to really check in with me, let alone come in and stand with me. More and more I thought about how the unusually large round pen allowed the horse to be far enough away from me that he felt just out of my reach, in a way. Sure, the flagging had some effect, and I could block him to change directions or put a little extra energy towards him to speed him up and so forth. Yet, I sensed that he knew when he stayed out there along the panels taking his thoughts out of the pen that I had little meaningful influence on him.

The third time I went out to work with him I decided to take out some of the panels and make the round pen smaller. After removing four of the 14 panels, the round pen felt a whole lot more cozy to me. It went from feeling too big to feeling almost a bit tight, now being a little smaller than the average round pen. With this smaller space, the gelding would not have a chance to feel he was successfully getting away from me; we would have a stronger constant overlap of the feel of one another. I got my flag and halter and went to the middle. The gelding went to doing what he always did, running along the fence looking like a llama with that head way up and those eyes looking far afield.

The change this time was rapid and very positive. I can't say for certain that the previous work hadn't been the ice-breaker and it was finally getting through to him that third day anyway, but within five minutes of some minor and well timed flag kerwhacks he turned towards me and walked right up to me and stood not looking like a llama. In fact, now I had to flag a little bit to block him from pushing on me as he approached.

Once he came up to me without pushing, I petted him on the schnoot keeping an eye on him that he kept his eye and thoughts on me—which he did—and then I walked off. The gelding came right along with me pretty as you please. A few minutes more and I was tipping his thought to either side and having him walk off and take several steps with me, then stopping and he'd turn and draw right back to me. The rather sudden positive changes felt like a real blessing after experiencing the previous session when I had to rope him to even get a halter back on him. Amazingly, his entire disposition changed and his posture along with it.

It wasn't all cleared up as he was plenty ready still to take his thought to the other horses if they made noise, and take off in their direction until the panels stopped him. But it was a profound and sudden change from where we began. And he was very able now to let go of those other thoughts and return to me in the pen. It seemed rather quickly he acknowledged that there was a growing good feeling between us and more and more readily he'd look me up and follow me with his head down and a softness that wasn't there previously.

The following session I worked with him saddled, and it went well, and the two sessions since then I have ridden the beast. The daughter of the owners also rode him after I did the last time I went out. There is work to do, but he is coming along letting go of those strong distracted thoughts and becoming more and more available to the requests of the reins, etc. It is looking like there is potential for him to be a decent riding horse.

To reflect again on this chapter's Harry clinic quote, the first part says, *"Few horses I meet are familiar with first being here."* And that's the key here with this gelding being rushy, worried, and impossible to catch or do much with. He was anything but "here" with me in the pen at first. But after getting beyond that spot to now where he is thinking "here" is a pretty good place to be, the relationship is turning out to be quite decent. Now if he can be convinced to always be "here first," then we ought to be able to go softly and happily "there" together.

CHAPTER NINETEEN

If You Don't Try Less...

Thursday, June 9, 2022—Mendin' Fences Farm in Rogersville, Tennessee.

"If you don't try less you'll never know if you had to do more," Harry said.

Now there's a quote to contemplate. Simple, and yet not so simple. And in a world of horsemanship where getting bigger in some way often is key to gaining a horse's attention and thus getting the activity and the relationship turning for the better, here Harry reminds us not to do too much.

Not so long ago I was working with a rider and her sensitive mare and this very thing came up. It proved to be a textbook example of what this chapter's quote is articulating. The mare often chomped the bit and was resistant to the reins and flung her head up and around when being ridden. After watching the pair display their riding for a few minutes I could see one root issue of the horse's lack of going along better with the person's requests on the reins.

"Stop shouting at her," I suggested.

"What?" the owner replied.

"The reins," I replied. "Try asking for what you want with

about 15% of the firmness you are putting on those reins."

She looked at me sort of funny, but then her expression softened and it seemed to click in her mind what I meant. She rode off and the next turn she made on her horse showed a horse with a decent bend all through her body, head down, and willingness to follow the rein without nearly so much of the junk that was present before.

It's not a very involved tale to tell. The results, however, were immediate and very exciting to see. The rest of the session, I observed the rider unintentionally fall back into her old heavy-handed habits only to catch herself in the act when her horse reminded her with tightness, resistance, and the busy mouth.

The mare was a fairly recent newcomer to the owner. The horse, of course, had her own background that played into the situation. She was an off-the-track Thoroughbred (you can imagine how the general use of the reins may have looked in that environment). Then the mare spent some years as a polo pony. I am suspicious that in that world riders rarely follow Harry's advice from this chapter's quote. The horse's background probably led to the mare appreciating someone speaking rather than yelling on the reins all the more. She really did seem to say, "Oh, thank you!" when the rider offered her requests very lightly on the reins. She was a sensitive thing.

Certainly, not all horses will present with such a magical turn-around in similar circumstances. But to discover whether or not greater intensity is required from us to get a job done, shouldn't we approach all horses with this chapter's quote in mind? I have often heard Harry mention the advice to always present a request to a horse as we would like it to be in its perfected, refined state first before escalating the bigness of the ask, if necessary. If we do not include this preliminary step in our asking, then horses are unable to know that there is a softer ask to which they can answer.

An easy ask must be offered initially so that horses may perceive it ahead of any escalation so that in the future they can recognize the easy ask and answer it to avoid the need for any intensification from the human. One component of this set-up is that horses begin to understand that it is in their own power to keep the human from getting unpleasantly bigger. It is as if they are training us to remain light and soft instead of the other way around. Consistency in presenting requests to horses this way can build a great deal of confidence in them to perform activities with us. If we approach all of our requests to horses this way, then even going into new territory is less likely to worry a horse so much—they get trained to think through whatever odd new thing we are doing to them and search out the answer rather than panic or worry that the new presentation from the human is a threat.

What often happens with humans is, especially in the beginning when we know intuitively that a horse has no frame of reference for what we are asking (like backing up off the feel on a lead rope or thinking along with a rein when we offer feel on it), the person skips that soft ask where we would like to end up because we know that there is no way the horse is going to hear it and react to it. So, the person goes right to a bigger ask to get the job done. And it works. And we do it again, and it works. So we just keep on going with it, because it works. It can become established that the person never considers trying the ask in any different way since it always works fine like this, at least to our sensibilities. But what if the horse is able to respond to a lighter request? An unnecessarily big ask can in fact become a barrier between a person and the horse—the horse reacts negatively to some extent to the assault of what amounts to a yell rather than being able to simple hear the person's request and willingly go with it.

I remember one time in particular when Harry elaborated on this subject during a clinic discussion with a little anecdote that I found particularly helpful in explaining the matter. Harry said to think about sitting in a seat in a movie theater and someone wants to slide past you to another seat but you are turned away from this person's approach talking to a friend. Think of the difference in how you would feel if the person grabbed your shoulder and shook you hard to say, "Hey, you—get out of my way!" or if that person barely touched your shoulder to ask politely to get your attention to slip past you. You are likely to be perfectly willing to adjust your legs or perhaps even stand up so that the other person can pass along the aisle if you simply are made aware of the situation. But being gruffly shook with more force than necessary puts you on the defensive and can have an immediate and lasting negative feel regarding the other person. That seems to fit well with this quote and certainly with what I saw happening with the horse and rider in the earlier example.

This chapter's thought really isn't rocket surgery (as some of my family would say). It is more of a reminder of a simple principle that can make a rather profound difference in a horse's response and responsiveness. And part of this one that I take away from considering it is that awareness is all important to better horsemanship. When I watched the rider and her horse in the above example, it was plain as day for me to see that the horse was sensitive and overwhelmed by the firmness she put on the reins. But, there are times where I catch myself doing the same thing on a horse I have been riding for some time. My awareness can become lost in the mire of me focusing on the task rather than how I ask the horse to perform the task. Then when I adjust my approach to a fraction of the intensity I was offering previously, the horse appreciates it and performs with more relaxation and willingness. It's a great bit of advice to keep in mind with whatever we are doing with our horses.

CHAPTER TWENTY

Clearing Out the Worry

Tuesday, August 24, 2021— Bible/Horsemanship Clinic, Floyd, Virginia.

"You can pet your horse carefully for 20 years and one day you make a fast move and he'll flinch," Harry said.

This chapter's quote reflects a situation that I had to learn and I am very glad the lesson came early in my horsemanship journey, once I met Harry. Also, it points to a problem that I come across all the time when working on horsemanship with horse owners. In particular when looking at the quick quip above, Harry using the word "flinch" gets me thinking.

An example related to this quote presented itself recently. I originally helped a client with her horse about three years ago. One of her horses had been with her for over a decade and then, in what seemed like a rather sudden change for no apparent reason to the owner, the gelding would not allow her to halter him.

The horse was kept in a stall some of the time and also enjoyed plenty of turn-out into a large pasture with other horses each day. In neither place was the owner now able to approach the horse and halter him. When outside, the horse simply moved away from her. In the stall, the gelding would posture in ways to keep his head out of her reach. The owner felt a bit threatened when working with him—not because the horse was directly threatening in his behavior per se, but rather that he could get pushy and reactive out of fear if she approached him too assertively.

Moving the horse from here to there and feeding the horse was easily enough accommodated without a halter given the layout of the barn and fences. Not being able to halter him for the trimmer, vet, any number of other important tasks, or an emergency, however, proved to be a problem. By the time I was called in, the issue had been going on for the better part of a year.

In our first session, I discovered quite a fearful horse was underlying the new behavior. I entered his stall with a halter and lead rope. The gelding tensed up and turned away from me and stuck his head in a corner of the stall. With the horse's butt to me, I got a little busy with the rope and halter against my chaps. This worried the horse more and he fidgeted. I dialed up the intensity of my busy-ness just to the point that the gelding searched for what to do next and then made the choice to try something different from what he was doing. He shuffled around and quickly stuck his head out the upper half of a stall door—two stall doors were positioned opposite one another that had open upper halves; one led to a pasture outside and one to an aisle way in the barn.

At first, he kept avoiding me by turning away from me in the tight confines of the stall. I continued to disallow those spots to work out by getting a little busy with the lead rope against my chaps, not in a big way that increased his anxiety to the point of acting in self-defense but with just enough of an ask to have him try something and not be stuck. I was getting it set up so that none of those head-away-from-me places worked out.

Getting the gelding to choose to turn and face me was the plan. Rather than chase him and attempt to catch his head to be haltered, as the owner had been trying to do, I wanted the horse to come to the decision to turn and face me. And I hoped for him to offer, or at least allow himself, to be haltered. Even though this horse was extremely worried about being caught, he had spent plenty of time in a halter in his life and I figured that once we got past this avoidance deal, most likely being caught and led would work out fine.

The gelding finally did chose to turn and face me. I was able to pet him on the face, at which point I walked away from him around the stall. He followed me. I stopped. He stopped with me. I petted him again. We went through the same thing once more and at that point I put the lead rope around his neck and then offered the halter and he was fine to be haltered. The whole business took about 10 minutes. The trouble really wasn't about the haltering per se, but had to do with getting the horse to let go of the thought of avoiding being there with the person, and especially of being caught and confined by the person. The horse was not relaxed by any means, but he seemed a lot less worried than when he was hoping to get away from my "hellos" by sticking his head into the corners and out of the doors.

Sizing-up my new client and discussing her horse problem, it was evident that she was rather apprehensive towards approaching the gelding. It was easy to see that the horse had worried her and she tip-toed around him like approaching him might get her killed. This clearly had worked out well for the gelding in the sense that he was looking not to be haltered. But at the same time, her timid approach seemed to have him even more worried than he might otherwise have been. It was as if she was telling him with her body language that there was something to be worried about and he believed it!

At the same time, it was apparent that she loved the horse and no-doubt had spent plenty of time being affectionate towards him. That must have produced plenty of good feeling interactions between them over the years. Taking into consideration her adoring demeanor towards the gelding, why would the horse not be willing to come to the nice lady who would rub on him with tons of doting strokes?

The simple answer I chalked up to the horse's history commingled with inconsistency regarding getting the gelding to bring his mind to the owner. The horse no-doubt originally came to this owner with some baggage from training and other experiences with humans. The critter presented as dubious of humans in such a strong way in general that I am convinced that he had good reasons to be; there was a certain palpable baseline of worry in this horse most likely founded in past bad experiences. That can be hard for a horse to overcome and difficult for a person to help a horse to sort out.

In the stall, I had presented myself big enough to get the horse to let go of his evasive distractions and to begin to think about me to the point that he turned and faced me. The owner on her own had been unable to get the horse mentally with her in this way. This was the key issue. Another part of the story was that the owner, although an experienced rider and horse person, did not understand how to offer a horse a feel to follow. This left her with driving the horse around or otherwise trying to make the horse do things. Moving a horse around in such mechanical ways does not really get a horse focused on you and isn't really what one would call a relationship.

Also, driving and trying to control a horse when you are at the core afraid of the horse—well, the horse picks up on this stuff. She never got a change in the horse that drew his attention to her and produced a willingness to come along with what she asked.

The event or situations that convinced the gelding to become impossible to catch and halter was unknown to the owner. I only can speculate on this, but I have a sense that something happened with the horse that dredged up some pretty bad feelings about humans from years earlier. Perhaps the evasiveness was a return to a behavior from when he was younger? Or maybe he just said heck with it; he wasn't going to allow himself to be haltered and in that way the problem was nipped in the bud? Whatever the reason, it was working and had become well established. No halter had been on him in months, and the pesky human would give up and go away to boot.

Long story shortened, when it was the owner's turn to try getting the horse with her and haltered in the stall, she was able to do this. After some practice over a couple of lessons, she began to accomplish this on her own without me there to coach her through it. The haltering issue seemed resolved.

But—and this is a really big but—once haltered, we played with some ground work with the gelding. So much worry and tension could be seen in asking even the smallest thing of this horse that he definitely needed to get to a better point in general about interacting with humans to help the situation. I would walk towards him a little matter-of-factly, not doing anything out of the ordinary, and he'd get bug-eyed and either stiffen up with his head way in the air or simply leave town at a high rate of speed and hit the end of the lead rope. What a miserable way to be, especially by default. He was terrified of interacting with humans.

This brings me back to Harry's quote, "*You can pet your horse carefully for 20 years and one day you make a fast move and he'll flinch.*" The owner had been tip-toeing around this horse for more than a decade, and one fast move—even something seemingly mundane—and not only did he flinch, but he took evasive maneuvers in a near panic.

"Petting the horse carefully" got the owner nowhere in terms of helping the gelding get to a better place where he could relax around people. Rather, it took more of an assertive approach, and one that began to ask something of the horse before the horse was able to realize that he could be okay around a person asking some things of him. We worked on approaching the horse many different ways and convincing the horse that these matter-of-fact interactions were not going to kill him. He made progress, and so did she. And with the haltering issue sorted out, eventually she felt she had a grip on things and we wrapped up the lessons.

The way Harry worded this chapter's quote makes me think

about his choice to use the word "flinch." He could have said, bolt or rear or something that denoted a larger reaction, as is the case with our example horse in this chapter. But no, Harry chose to say flinch. I think this is important because it shows clearly that even a tiny bit of reaction when approaching your horse to do something as seemingly pleasant as pet him demonstrates that worry and tension are present. If the horse flinches at your touch in perfectly calm and wonderful conditions, how is that going to look when there is some real stress involved? It almost certainly will look a whole lot bigger. The little things we gloss over are what become the big things that we can't miss and get us and our horses in real trouble. And tip-toeing around it doesn't help the horse to feel better. The worry is not cleared out until we prove to the horse he need not worry about our approaching him. And to accomplish this we have to take the horse to those places and prove that it's okay.

So much could be said on this subject...but let me wrap up by returning to the example. Just recently, and three years on from what I already described, I got a call from the client. The vet came out and had floated the gelding's teeth—a difficult situation due to the horse's angst and one that required three rounds of sedation this time—and ever since, she again was unable to halter him, again.

This horse is a tough case, granted. But the fact remains that when she went to pet the horse over the past few years since our initial work, most certainly he flinched some of the time, even at a pleasant approach and touch. The owner still was tip-toeing around the gelding when I went back to work with her again. But, she is doing a great job now, being re-focused on getting the horse's mind with her and getting the horse okay to draw to her, be haltered, and be approached and touched. The situation with the horse's regression after the teeth floating ordeal has the owner very keen to see if she can get him to a much better spot and she is working very hard to follow through and do that.

Now, it seems that the horse's little flinches are much more visible to the owner. I know that she desperately wants the horse to feel better around her and people in general. Reprogramming ourselves to see more and to act differently to break certain habits is at the heart of getting positive changes in our horses, and that's the real challenge. Becoming able to see those little flinches as early warning signs and to be able to address them, clear them out, and build that better relationship with our horses is key. Being careful to avoid the uneasy spots in horses may momentarily avoid an escalation in worry, but it doesn't relieve the worry and clear it out. And worry about a human's approach is a barrier to a better relationship with horses.

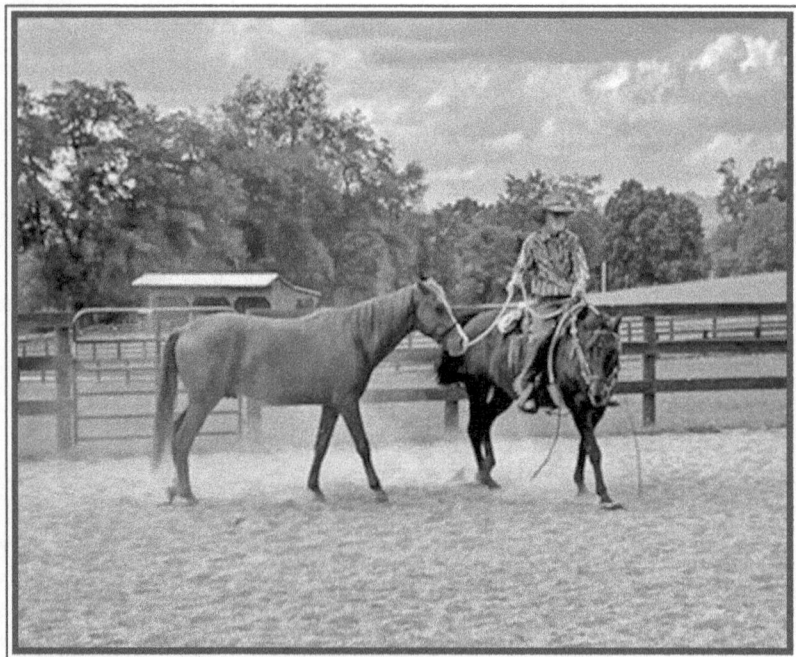

Riding Mirage and ponying Newly is looking pretty good in this photo from August 24, 2023 during Week Two of the Bible/horsemanship clinics in Floyd, Virginia. But shortly before this nice moment, I had to spend quite a bit of time in the saddle getting Mirage more with me and lessening her focus to kill Newly! Newly had no previous experiences being ponied and seemingly in no way comprehended that any other horse might not like him. Succeeding with such a challenge makes me extremely grateful for the time I have been able to spend filling these clinic journals and learning from Harry and from horses. The kind of together moment shown in this photo also is the sort of progress I hope my writing may help others to achieve with their horses. (Photo: Jaime McArdle)

CHAPTER TWENTY-ONE

Pet Her and Leave

Tuesday, August 14, 2023—Bible/Horsemanship Clinic, Floyd, Virginia.

"Most people when they get that thought centered, they want to keep that thought there for a long time—but when you get that thought centered, pet her and leave," Harry remarked.

Sometimes when we humans do manage to get a horse's thought with us we may soak up the joyous moment too long and the horse's mind (and sometimes the body with it) checks out in the midst of our victory cuddle. It is helpful to keep in mind that when a horse looks you up, what comes next is every bit as important to building with-you-ness as is getting the horse's focus in the first place. We can wear out our welcome pretty quick with a horse who has struggled to get her mind with the human.

A moment-by-moment reality is flowing when working with horses. How those moments unfold, of course, is going to effect how things go with the horse over time. A big take away from this quote is that there is a "shelf life"—especially at first—to the attention span of horses who are not accustomed to having their minds here and centered on us humans.

To have the greatest positive impact on getting horses' minds centered on you at first, one needs to keep the encounter brief. Then look to draw or direct the horse to do something, and repeat getting the focus centered up as necessary. One might get big enough to get a horse to focus, then pet his face, and then walk off and just see if there is enough good feeling there to have the horse follow. (This is what Harry was talking about during the session when this quote was spoken.) If not, there's more work to do. If so, then halleluiah, and perhaps you can stop again and pet the horse if she remains centered with you. But, if you stay there too long and the horse is unable to maintain with you then her attention expiration date shows up and the horse leaves you before you leave first to draw her or try to direct her to what to do next.

It is advisable to set things up so that the horse doesn't get in the habit if deciding she is done with paying attention to you and goes off. Rather, if the human can be directing things with the horse all along, then the habit becomes that the horse has her mind centered there with the person, and her own body, and that it feels good to the horse to be present and to follow.

Another quote is written in my clinic journal that Harry spoke soon after this chapter's opening quote. He said, "If I can get the thought here strong enough long enough then she'll line her body up here."

There's a bit packed into this statement. As we've mentioned, just getting the horse's thought here with the person at all is a big goal. If it is a very distracted horse and a very brief moment of focus with the person, it at least creates a blip where the horse's mind isn't so far gone and that usually has a positive and settling upshot to it. Build on that with many moments of focus and the trend is for the horse to realize that having her mind centered feels better than all of the worry and distractions. Eventually, as Harry points out, "she'll line her body up here." That is, in this instance, the horse will line her body up straight to you rather than coming in to you crooked or at an angle because her mind is really drawing all of her to you.

At some point, as the person gets it so that the horse's thought is directable, we can see this come into play in many areas. Trailer loading is one of my favorite places to see this aspect demonstrated. There is perhaps no greater example of a crooked horse then one who is not thinking about getting into a trailer when a person is asking her to.

Years ago I was hired to help a horse owner with a giant Warmblood who wouldn't load and who was a fabulous example of a horse thinking strongly about anywhere but in the trailer when it was time to load. I was told that the show horse had been an okay loader before going to a trainer for 15 months, in which time it seemed he had been trained extremely well to not load, and pretty much try to kill the owner in the process of not loading. The owner explained that even the sight of the trailer was enough to send this horse into conniption fits. I said sure, I'd come and see if I could help.

When I arrived, a gooseneck trailer—a two horse straight-load with a ramp, behind a tack room—was hooked to a pickup out in a spacious graveled parking area outside an equally spacious barn. I suggested that the owner get the horse from the barn and show me how things went when she attempted to load the horse.

She disappeared into the barn and returned leading a 17 hand giant. She led him right to the open trailer and got about half way up the ramp when the shenanigans began. The gelding was all kinds of crooked, head up, prancing, and generally providing an excellent example of a horse with completely uncentered thoughts. But the wrestling match only lasted about 20 seconds before he reared, spun around in the direction of the owner nearly clocking her in the head, ripped the rope from her hands, and galloped full tilt across the parking lot and disappeared back into the barn.

"See what I mean?" the owner asked.

I did.

I asked if I could give it a shot, and she said, "By all means."

I walked to the barn to retrieve the horse and was met by a

woman who was leading the rogue back out to us.

"You lose a horse?" she asked.

"Why, yes!" I replied, gratefully accepting the rope that she happily handed me.

I began leading the horse towards the trailer, but stopped a few times to back him and get his mind centered with me as the horse already had a mind disappearing from me at the task of just being led. By the time we got about 20 feet from the trailer ramp, he was leading quite nicely.

I stopped and then asked the horse to circle me. Boy, did that interrupt the brain of the Warmblood that already had gone off to the ether again just by stopping. He reared and raced, and I interrupted with some big whacks of the lead rope end against my shotgun chaps. He'd look at me and I'd pet him a stroke down the nose. But I didn't keep him there looking me up for long. Pretty quickly I would asked for a circle one way or the other, then center his mind with me again and pet him. Next, I'd back him up, see if he could come forwards straightly, then stop, and pet him on the face a stroke. I'd let him stand a moment, then circle me again.

Within a couple more minutes, he had let down a ton. Now, he was able to, with his mind not bouncing around like a pinball in an arcade on Saturday night, focus on me and what I asked. In this instance where the horse was tremendously dramatic, it amazed me how quickly he came through. I chalked it up to the horse really wanting to feel better and be handled in a way that he could be mentally present and thereby let down and follow a person. It was as if the bad behavior drama had an equally wonderful willing and gentle giant side, and he flipped quickly between the two.

So, five minutes into the ground work and Mr. Warmblood was calm, standing still, head down, and pretty darn relaxed. I offered that we walk towards the trailer; the horse came along with no resistance whatever or even seeking a distraction. I stopped by the left edge of the trailer ramp and stayed standing on the ground and asked him to think up in the trailer and walk on in. He did so without hesitation, just as pretty as you please, straight as an arrow into the trailer all the way, and he stood there calmly.

I petted his bum and looked over at the owner.

She appeared to be somewhere between amazed and infuriated. But there we had an excellent example of a horse who was able to line his body up fine because I got his thought "here."

Reflecting on this chapter's quote, at first, I definitely had to get his mind centered with me, pet him, and then go to ask something else of him right away or he surely would have had time to bounce his brain off to somewhere else and get wound up again. Often, horses who don't know much about getting their minds centered up with a human—an indeed have the habit of the exact opposite—simply can't handle much of it even when we are successful at getting their brains here with us and it is a positive experience for them. These micro-moments are, however, greatly beneficial if they are brought into being and then we move off to draw the horse. And horses do take notice of them and it allows them to start to realize there's a better way to be with a person.

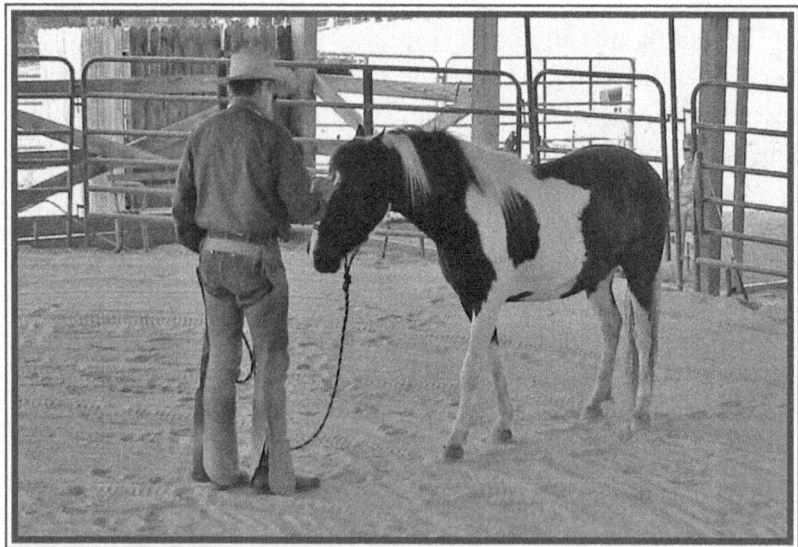

Harry often will give a quick pet to a horse during a session like this one from June 15, 2015 at Mendin' Fences Farm in Tennessee.

CHAPTER TWENTY-TWO

There's a Difference

Tuesday, August 14, 2023—Bible/Horsemanship Clinic, Floyd, Virginia.

"There's a difference between looking and leaving the scene mentally," Harry explained.

The main objective to horsemanship, to my way of thinking, is discovering and implementing ways to get horses to relax in their interactions with humans that thereby foster a willingness to undertake what people ask them to do and thusly build happy relationships. The best (and only) means of truly achieving this, as I have learned from Harry Whitney, is to recognize when a horse's mind is not centered and present with his body and then to get that mind centered up and with you.

This chapter's quote provides some insight into that dreaded saying we hear in the better circles of horsemanship, "Well, that depends...."

With horses, stuff always depends. It does so because every horse and every situation is different. Doing something with this horse that produces the desired outcome in this situation may not be the thing to do with that horse in a very similar circumstance. What we see in different horses outwardly may look quite similar between a perfectly acceptable mindset and another that we want to avoid.

This short quote is its own answer to what Harry means; there is a difference between a horse merely looking at something across the way and the horse leaving the scene mentally. Other words can be put to the idea and we might say something like, "there's nothing wrong with a horse looking around and being aware of his environment—in fact, that is a good thing—but it becomes a problem if the horse gets so involved with whatever he is seeing that he can't let it go and return his focus to the human and/or the task at hand."

I have shared the story many times over the years in print, in interviews, and in lessons of my wife's sorrel gelding Niji and me early in my horsemanship journey having some specific troubles on our farm road. It seems a great example to share here, too, to provide some practical insights into this idea. Niji was the horse that triggered my horse obsession, and he was the horse that got me looking to get better with horses in the first place. I was very challenged to try and get some with-you-ness going with that gelding at first.

In this instance, I had failed epically to get things going well enough with him to go out and have a safe and fun ride pretty much anywhere outside of the round pen. We'd seem to get things going okay in the pen, and then I would go ride in the yard a little bit. That even went okay at times. But then, the next thing you know, off he'd go in some wayward direction through the woods or tearing across the yard, and I was at a loss to get him steered or stopped or pretty much anything that I wanted. My brilliant idea this time was to go back to the round pen and start from scratch and work at it for a long time until it was right. Really, really right. A total reboot, maybe, would do the trick.

I worked at this for quite some time—I am talking about more than month—until I hoped to be able to leave the round pen and go out to explore the big world of the farm here. Upon venturing out of the round pen, I rode several days close by in the yard and had no wrecks or mishaps. I was getting more than a little tickled and confident with my newfound success with the gelding, and I was convinced that my plan had worked.

Now, with Niji going great, it was time to go and enjoy a ride to the other side of the farm. A perfect precursor to a real trail ride. And it went so perfectly, too...at first. Along the farm road away from the house and round pen area we went. We dipped down into a valley. Everything went fabulously. I mean, he was right there humming along at a brisk walk without a single sidetrack. My delight soared to new heights. Finally, success!

Soaking up this joyful, victorious ride—me proudly atop the handsome sorrel—we climbed seemingly seamlessly as one creature up out of the valley and got to the top of the hill. At the top of the hill, there is a Y in the road. Left goes to the entrance to our place and Carol's Paint stallion Chief was living up there in a pasture. Right goes down a rougher old road along a border fence that eventually leads to a river. Did I mention that we got to a Y in the road? I simply indicated we were going to the left with a little feel on the left rein. Niji...well, Niji was more of a going to the right kinda guy at that moment, and he let me know it.

And there's where I noticed that we had a breakdown in communication. I kept up my request to go one way. Niji, being the bigger one of us, and the one with four feet on the ground, felt that surely he had the majority vote. With me feverishly working to get my way, he went sideways over ditches, backwards up banks, forward past trees with low hung branches (trying to scrub me off)...it was a pitiful mess! And a total regression showing the collapse of all of that hard work I had been doing for weeks on end.

I got down and did some ground work. Well, that's not exactly true. I got down, got as far away from him as the lead rope would allow, and had a really sizeable infantile fit, being completely undone and right back again where I had started. Then I tried to do some groundwork, which also looked a mess. But I got it the best I could under the circumstances with my soul sunk to the gutter again, and then walked him back home.

So, when I got Niji back to the house and put away, I called Harry.

In retrospect, I find this kinda funny as I can see just clear as day what was happening. But at the time, I had no clue. It certainly was one of those, "Until you see it you don't see it, and then when you do see it, you wonder how you never saw that before," things.

Harry suggested that I get someone to come over and watch me ride—someone who knew enough about when a horse's mind is with a person or not to tell me as I rode when Niji's mind wandered. I got Terry Wood, who was a trimmer friend of ours and who was the one who got me in touch with Harry in the first place, to come over and do that very thing. So I got on Niji and I started to ride away from the shed in his paddock where I had mounted. We started with a step towards the farm road. We went two steps and Terry said, "There he goes!"

"What? You've gotta be kidding?" I said.

"Nope, he's gone already," she reiterated.

Well, that was eye opening. Depressing, but eye opening. Not even three steps! But it explained a whole lot.

On the previous equine expedition where Niji and I got ¼ mile of brilliant ride in before the problems showed up, I had been stumped. Stumped as to why the ride went so perfectly for so far only to crash and burn at the top of that distant hill so quickly and utterly? What Terry pointed out to me was all the explaining necessary to figure that one out for myself, finally. Niji and I actually were no more together at any point along that trip than we were when the big tussle ensued. The difference earlier in the ride (when I was basking in the delight of my "success") was that Niji and I individually wanted to go to the same place at the same time. The truth was that we were in parallel universes. It didn't weigh a thing to go along with Niji then because both he and I wanted to go to the same place at the same time. But as Terry was pointing out, he was not with me. This had been the clincher all along, and more than a month of round pen work was not about to change it for the better if I was not able to see when his mind was with me or not. And then get it with me when it wasn't. And make it a good deal for the horse when it was.

Whew!

From that point on, I made it central to my riding to better know if a horse is with me—really with me—or not. When riding, that meant checking in with a horse more. Pick up a rein to see if the horse is there and letting go of whatever else might be going on and really hear that rein, for example. In ground work, there is the benefit of seeing more of the horse, seeing his eyes and his whole body, to better observe if his mind is wandering away and he is stuck on a distraction. But in every circumstance, I determined to do a better job of really grasping if a horse was mentally with me or not, whatever I had to learn to see and feel it.

When Harry said, "There's a difference between looking and leaving the scene mentally," he meant that there is a real disparity in the horse's mindset between those two realities. If a horse looks at a deer jumping a fence a little ways off, who can blame him? He is a hardwired flee from fear machine...of course he's going to look at that. So will humans. But, after he looks, spends a second of time to determine what it is and that it really is no threat, and you ask him back onto the task at hand, is he available to come back to you? That's the rub. Pick up a rein, and is there a softness that says, "Yes, I'm listening; what needs to happen next?" Or, is there a hardness in it that shows a resistance to you interfering with his important business of watching what's going on out there?

With Niji, he wasn't just looking—he was definitely wrapped up in those other things before I was able to discern the difference and do something about it. Even when we were "happily" going along "together" up the farm road at first, had I known how better to check in with him I would have discovered that he was looking up the road because he had his own agenda to go there. He was not following my lead to go there.

This chapter's simple quote does a fine job of capturing a

really important tool in the horsemanship toolbox. Recognizing if the horse is mentally here and available or gone off somewhere mentally is paramount to getting a horse more with you and getting him relaxed and willing. Quotes like this one really get me considering how a person can develop new understandings that lead to attaining better skills. Better skills, in turn, help to put practical means of attaining better and more willing relationships with horses in humans' hands.

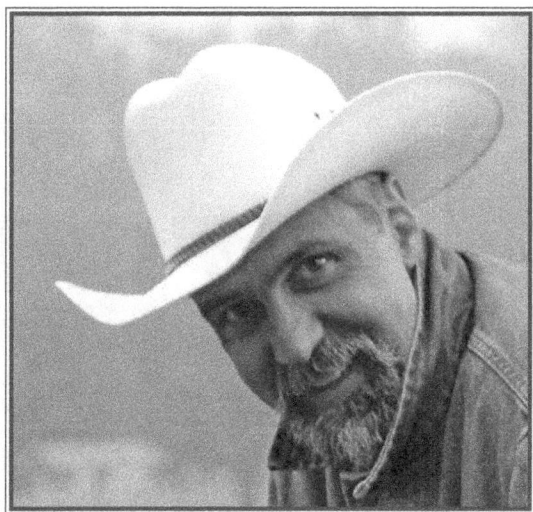

About the Author

Tom Moates is a leading equestrian author and journalist. This award winning writer is on the masthead of *Equus* magazine as a Contributing Writer, and his articles have run in many horse magazines in the United States and abroad including: *Eclectic Horseman*, *America's Horse*, and *Western Horseman*. Moates's previous books include the *Six Colts, Two Weeks* trilogy, and his other titles, *Discovering Natural Horsemanship, A Horse's Thought, Between the Reins, Further Along the Trail, Going Somewhere, Passing It On, Mane Thoughts*, and *Round-Up: A Gathering of Equine Writings*. Recently Moates took a foray into fiction and published *The Old Sleeper*, a spy novel (and yes, it does have horses in it). Moates lives on a solar powered farm with his wife Carol and a herd of horses in the Blue Ridge Mountains of Virginia. Book ordering info, horsemanship clinic and lesson info, and Moates's latest publishing news are available at www.TomMoates.com.